My Sweet

COLORING BOOK FOR ADULTS AND KIDS

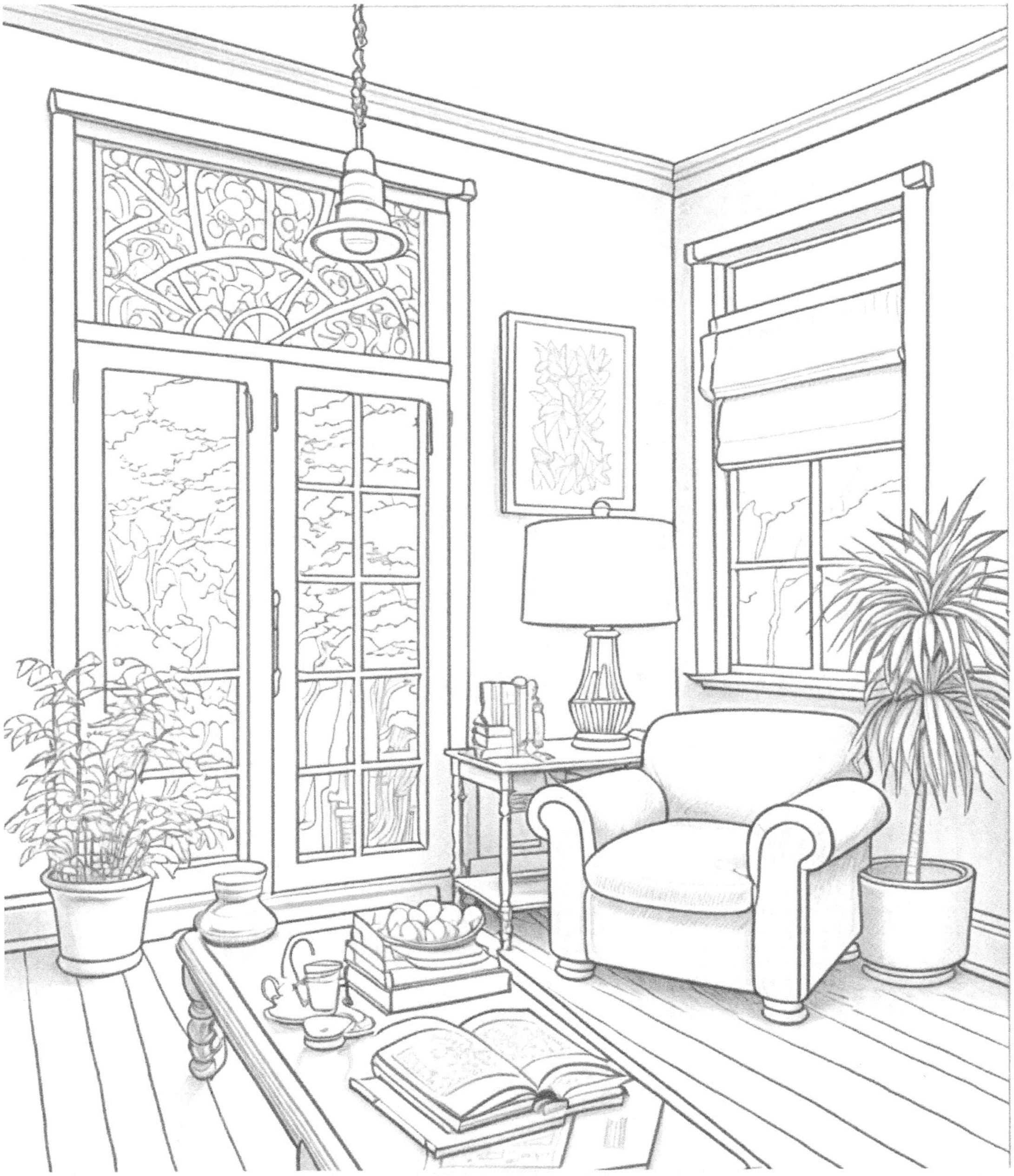

The Sunset

NOTEBOOKS AND BOOKS DESIGNING

COLOR TEST PAGE

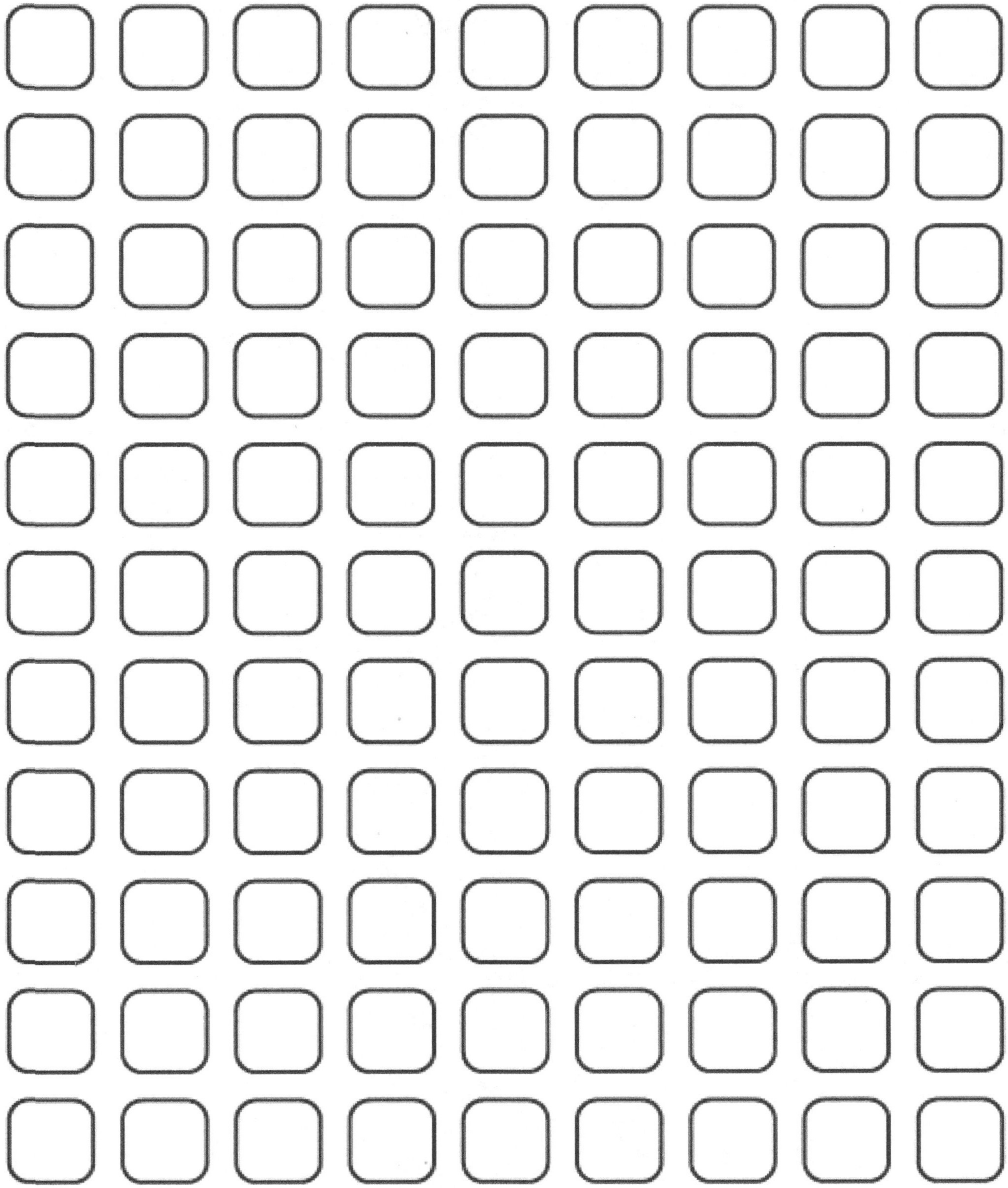

This Book belongs to:

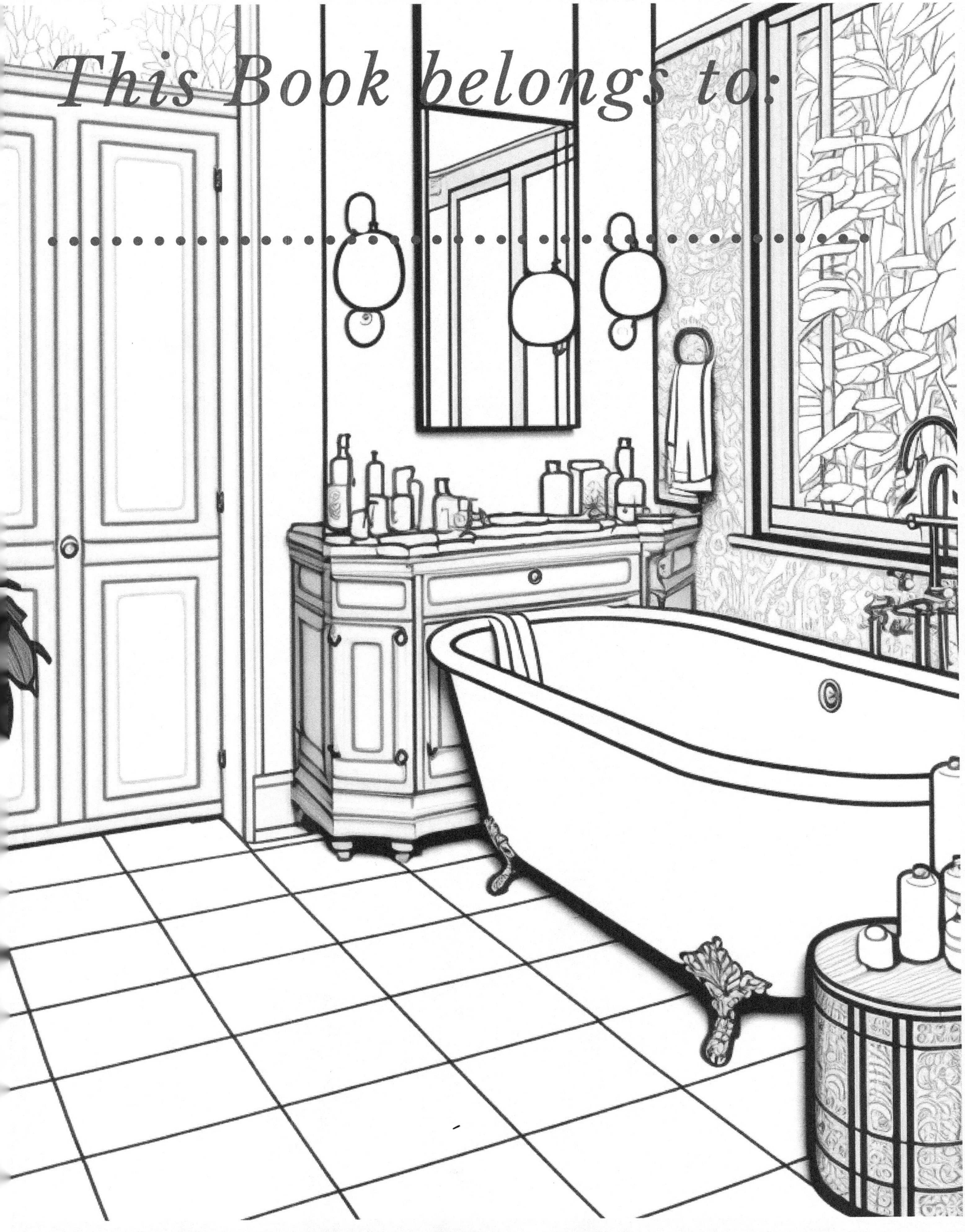

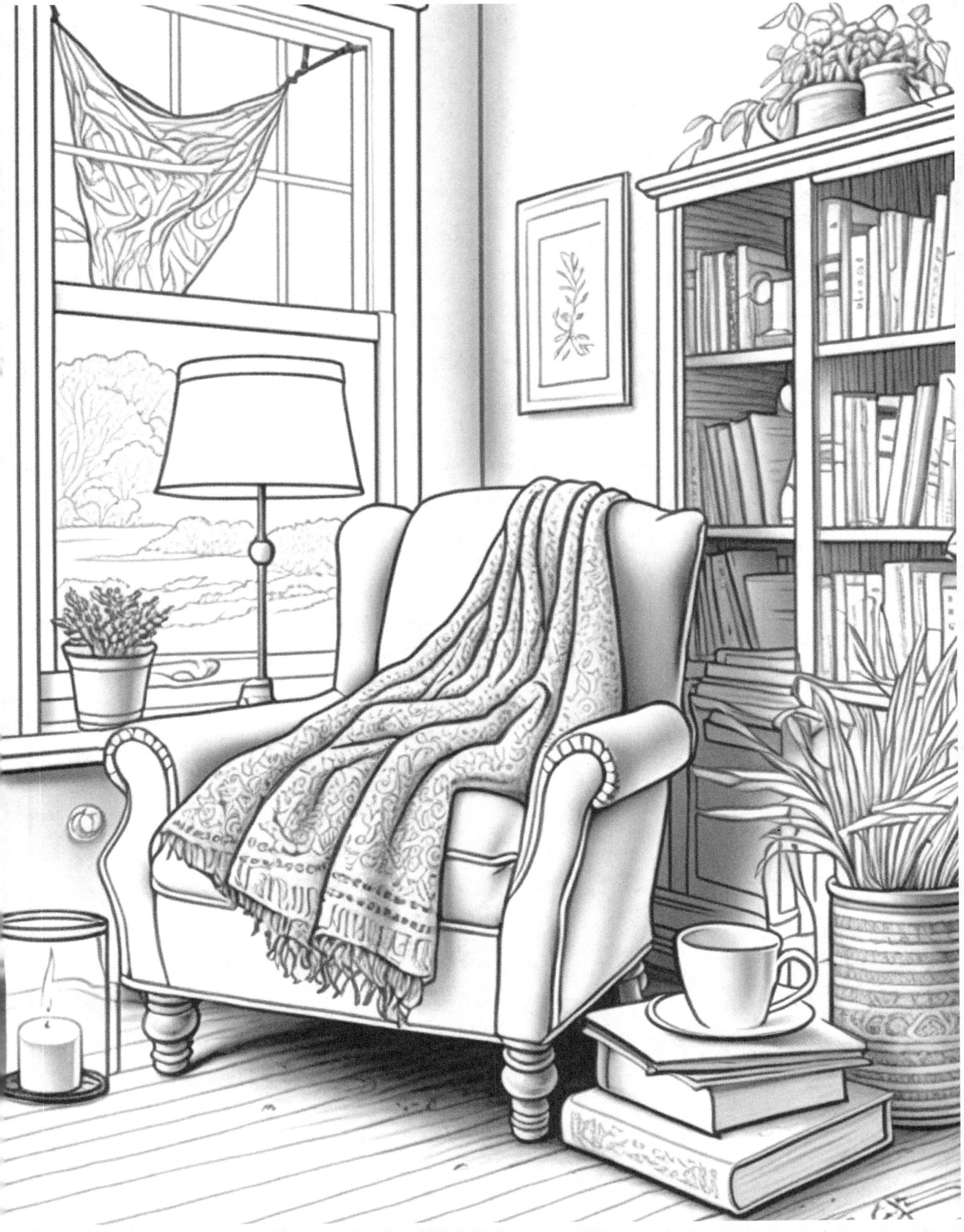

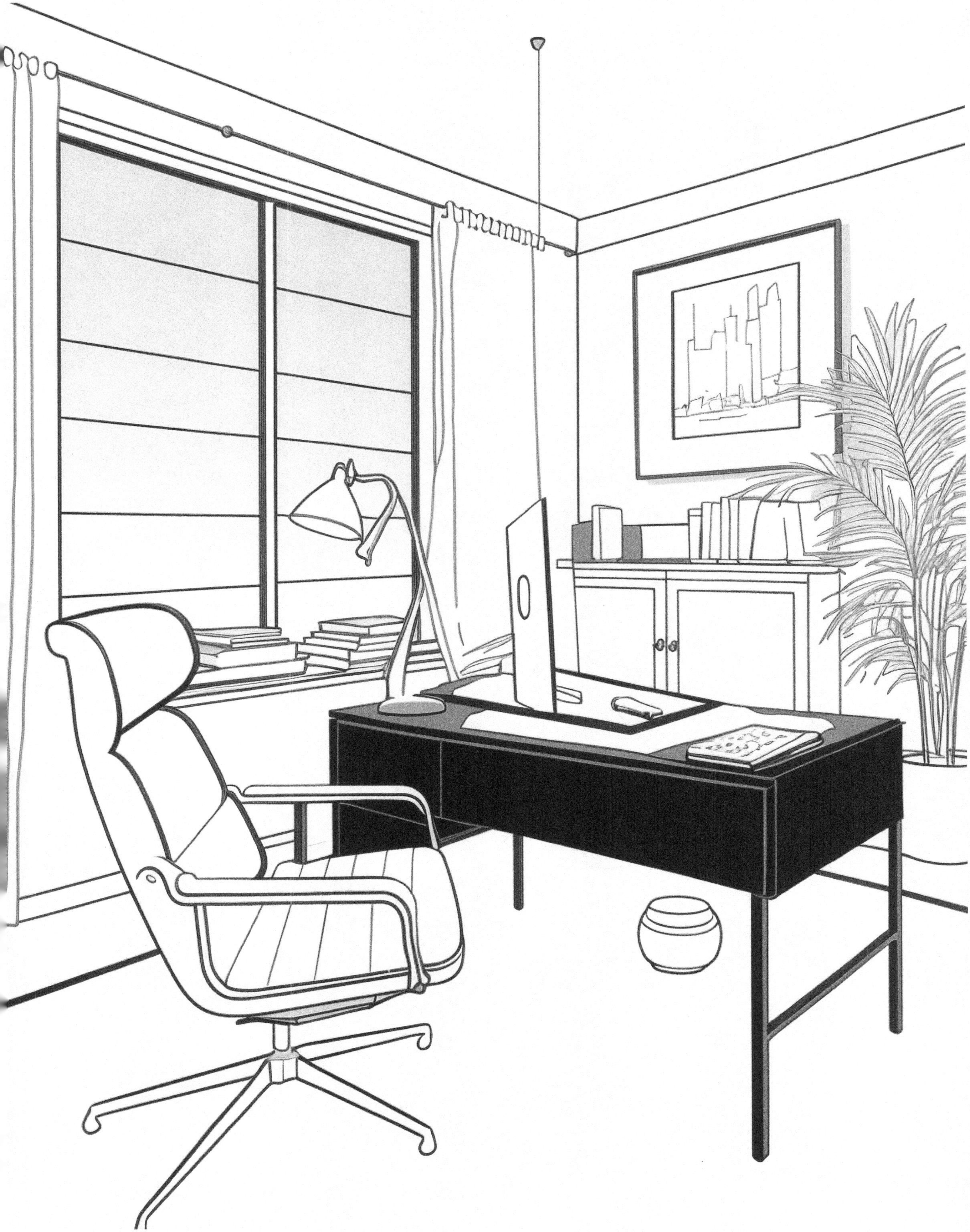

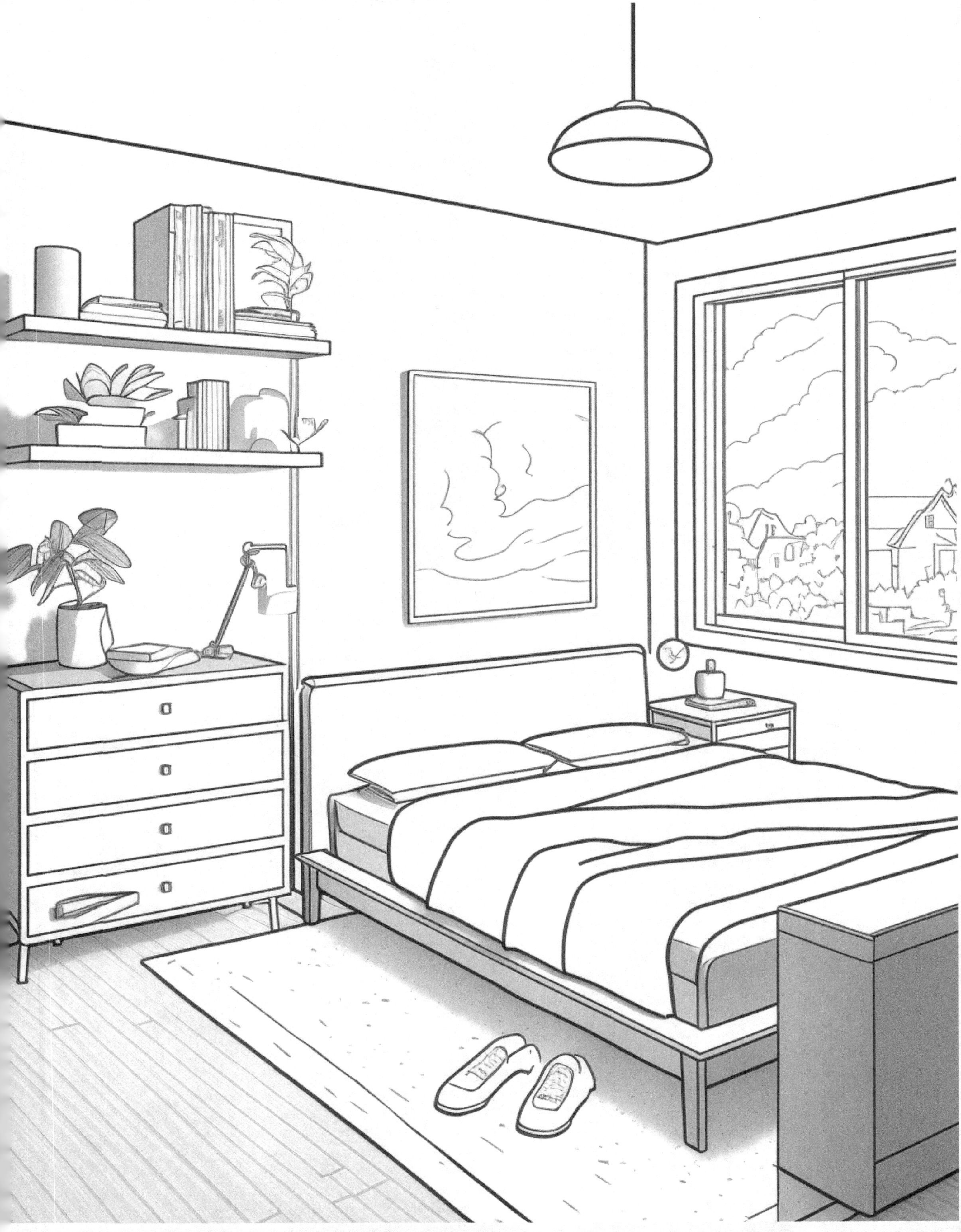

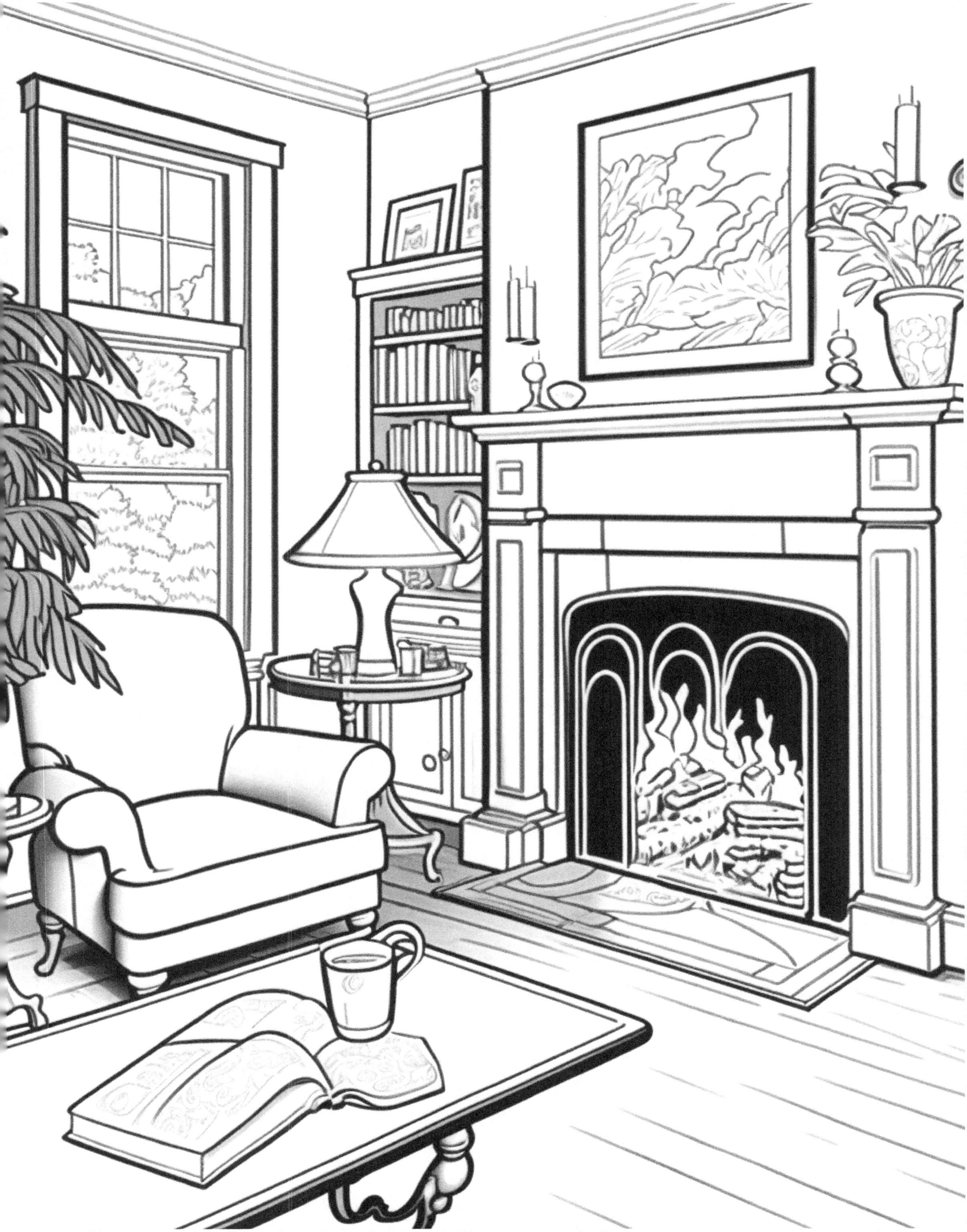

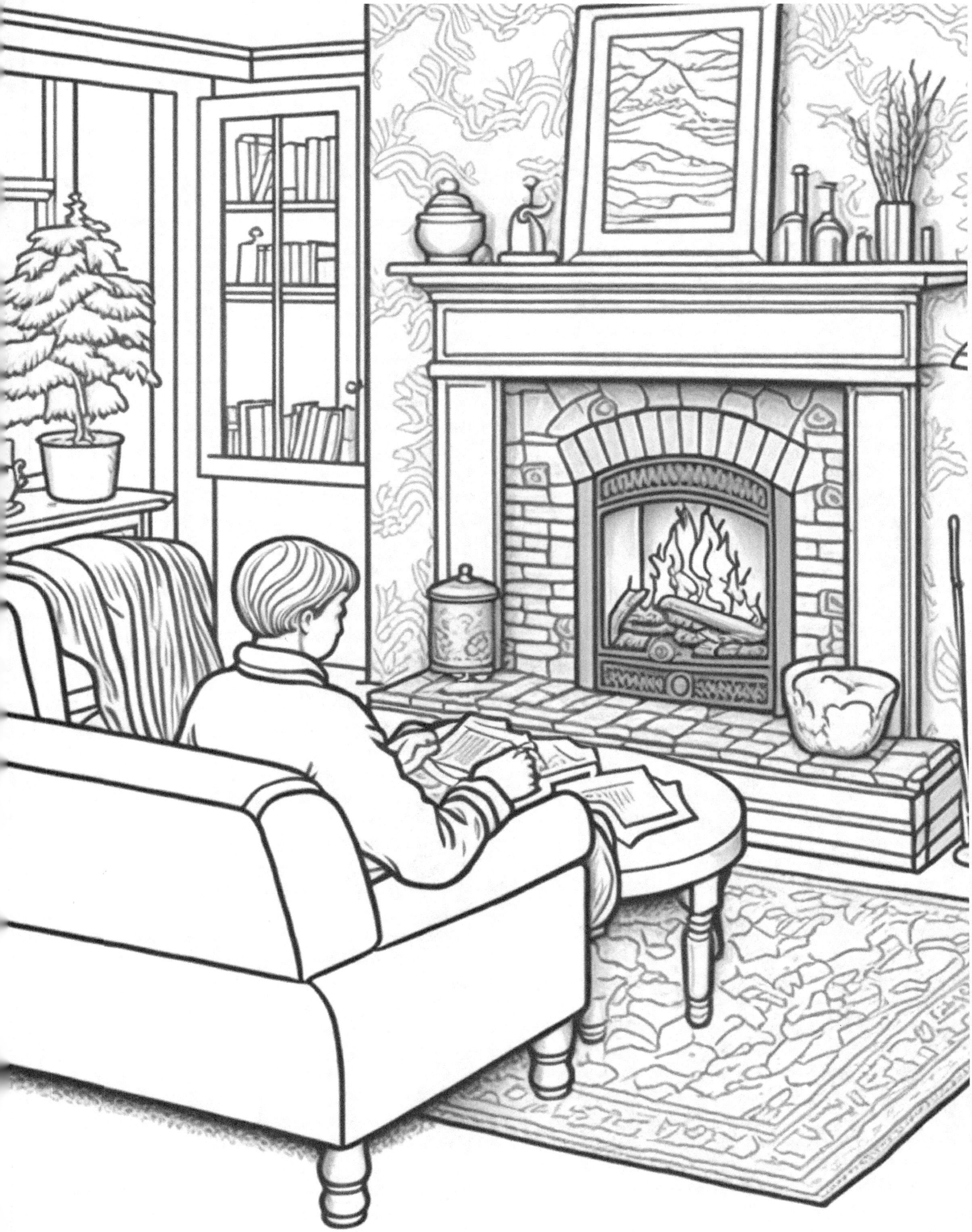

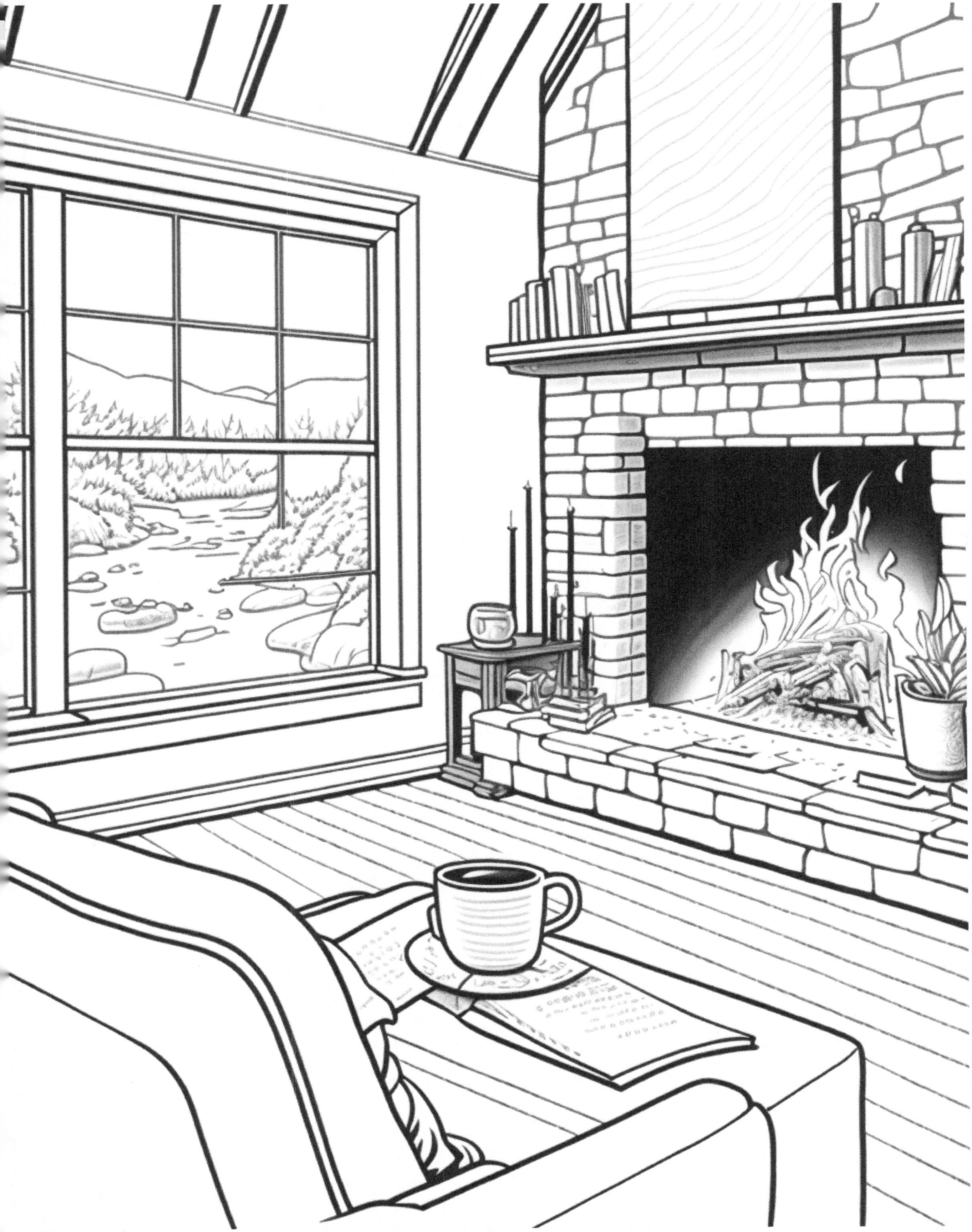

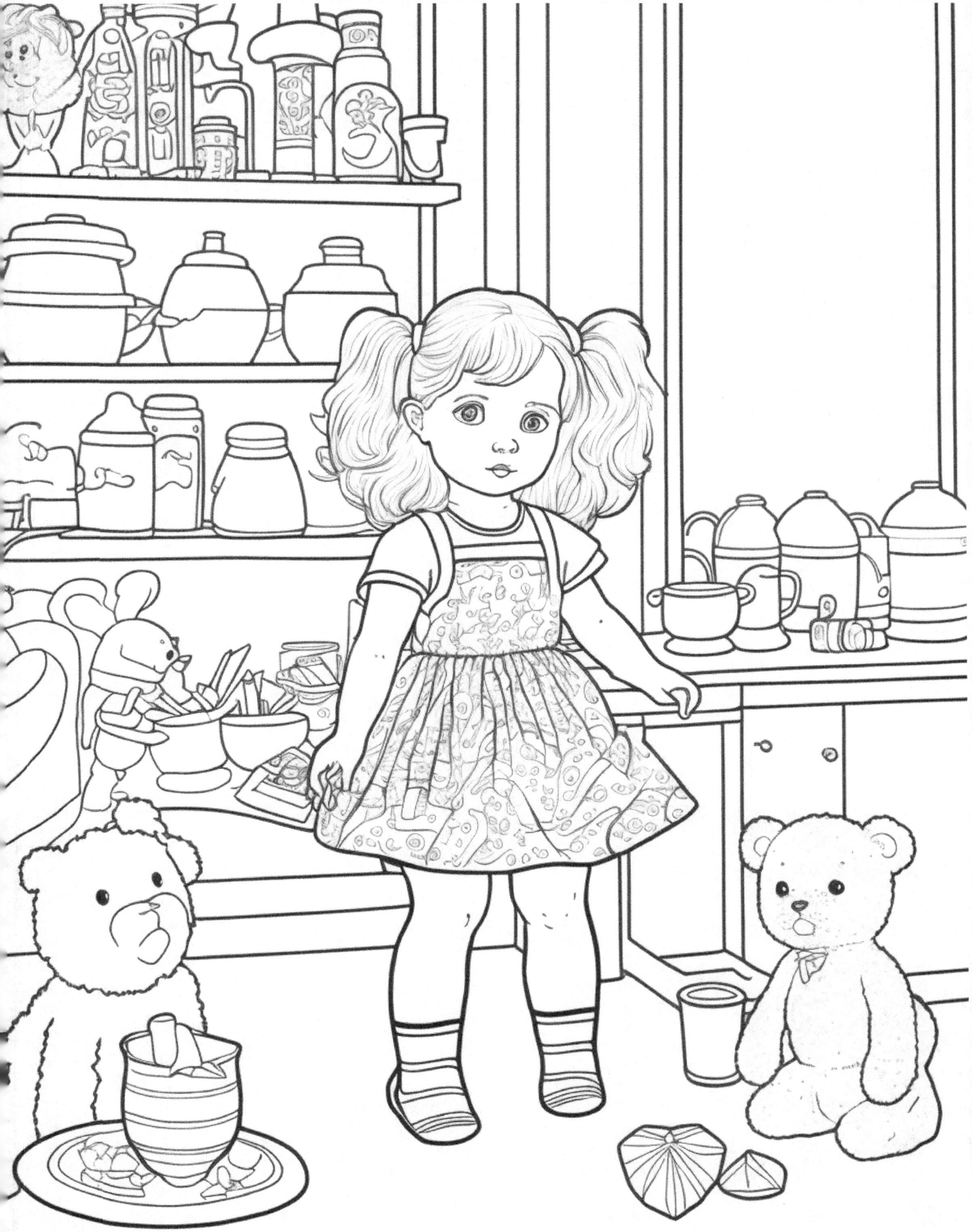

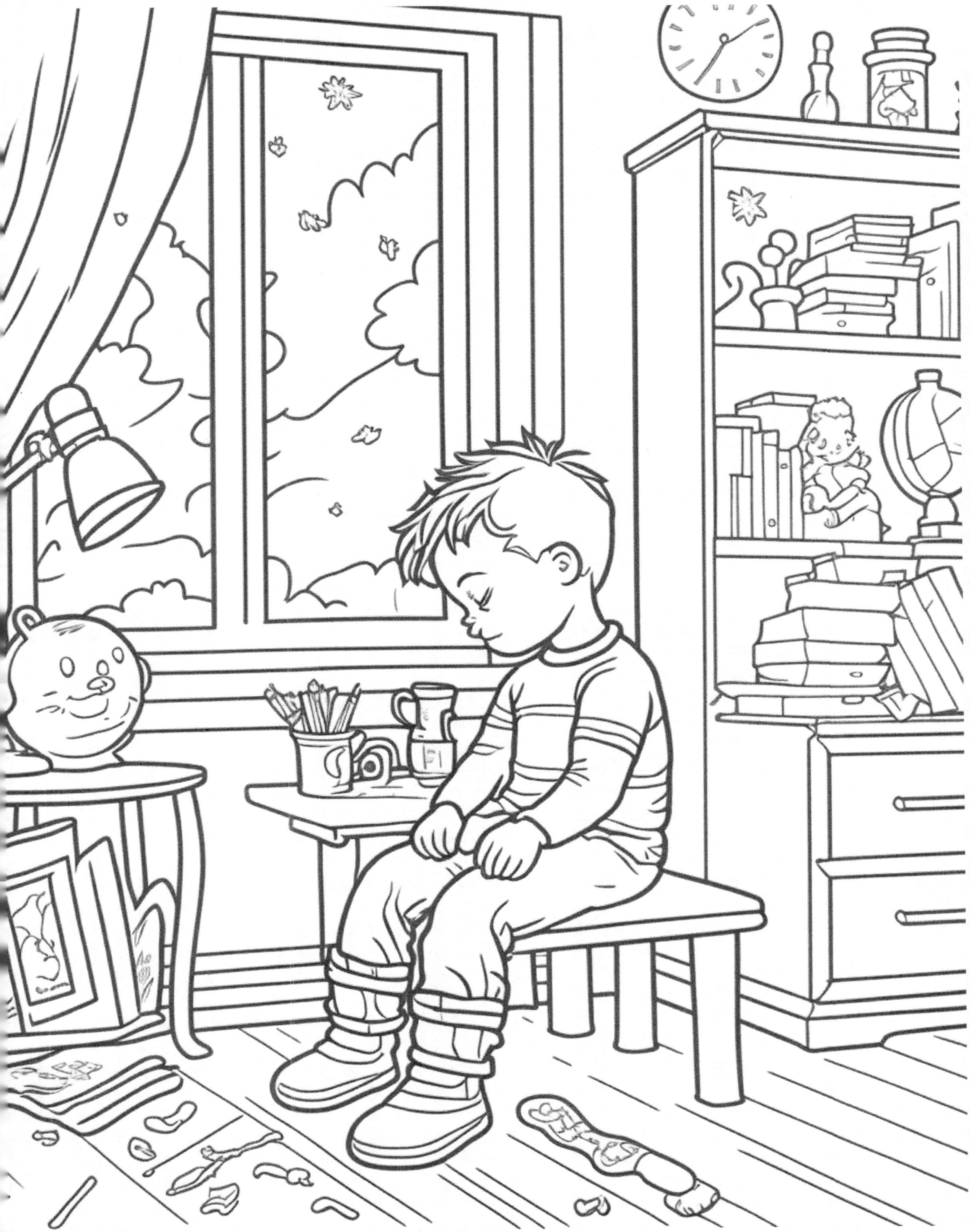

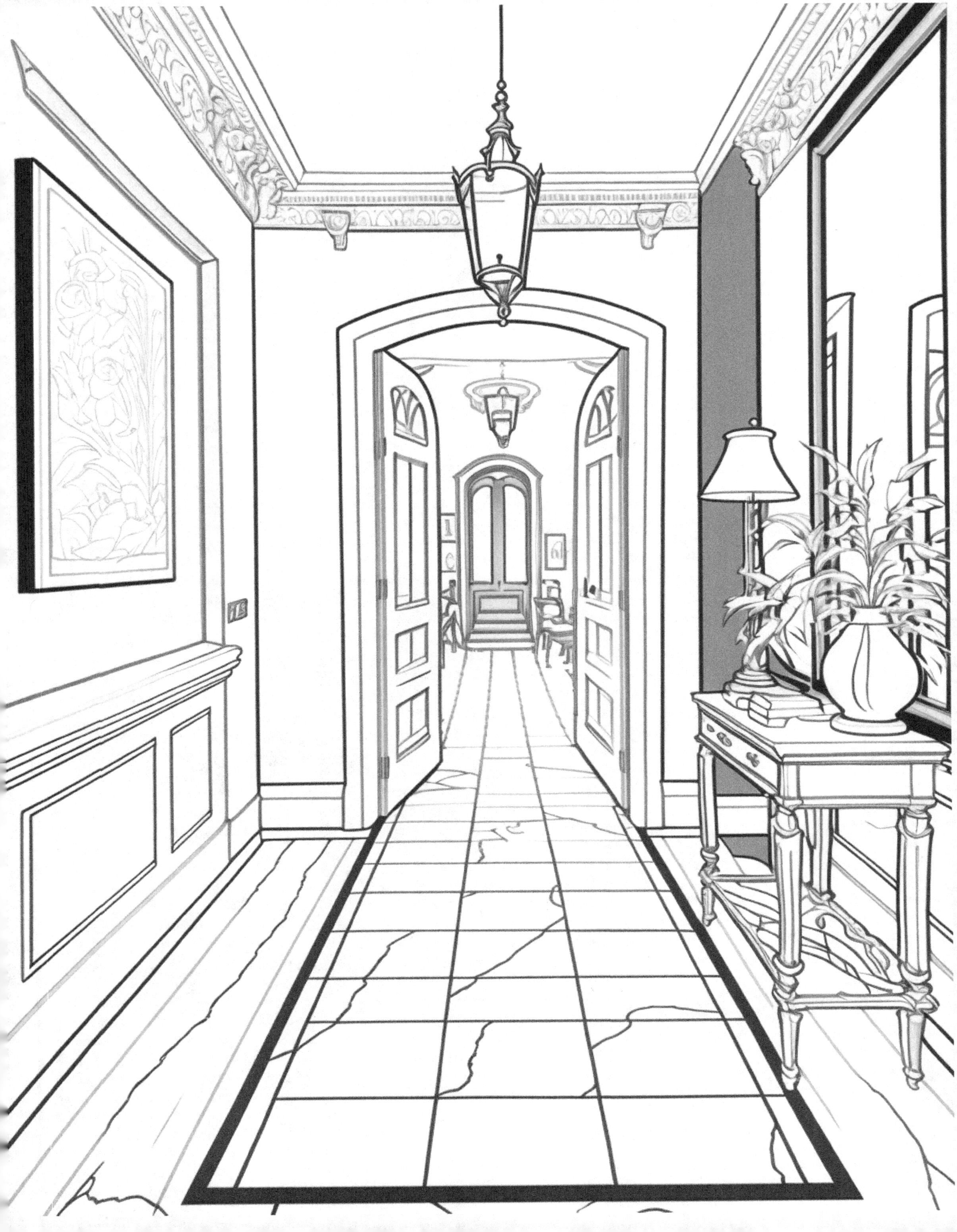

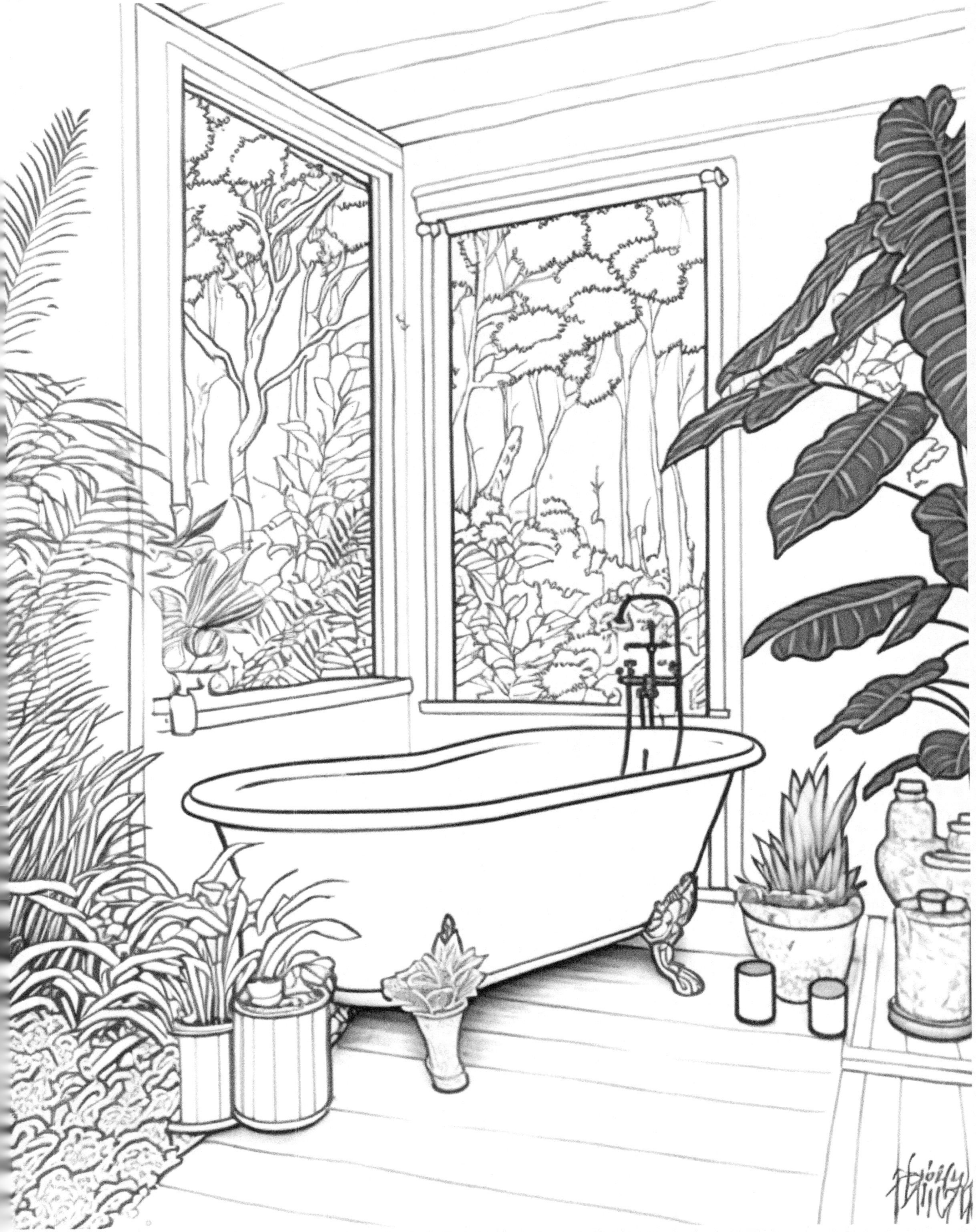

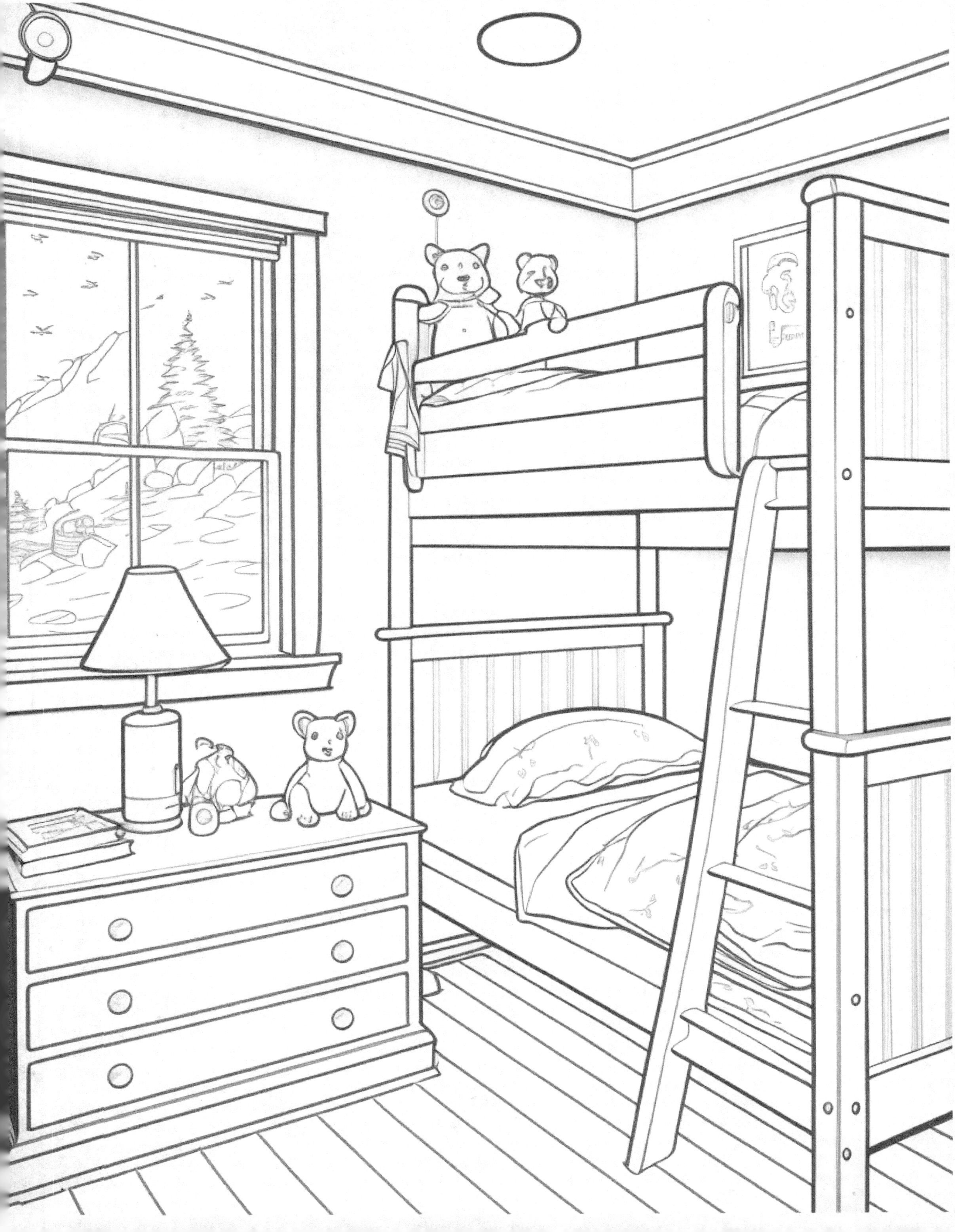

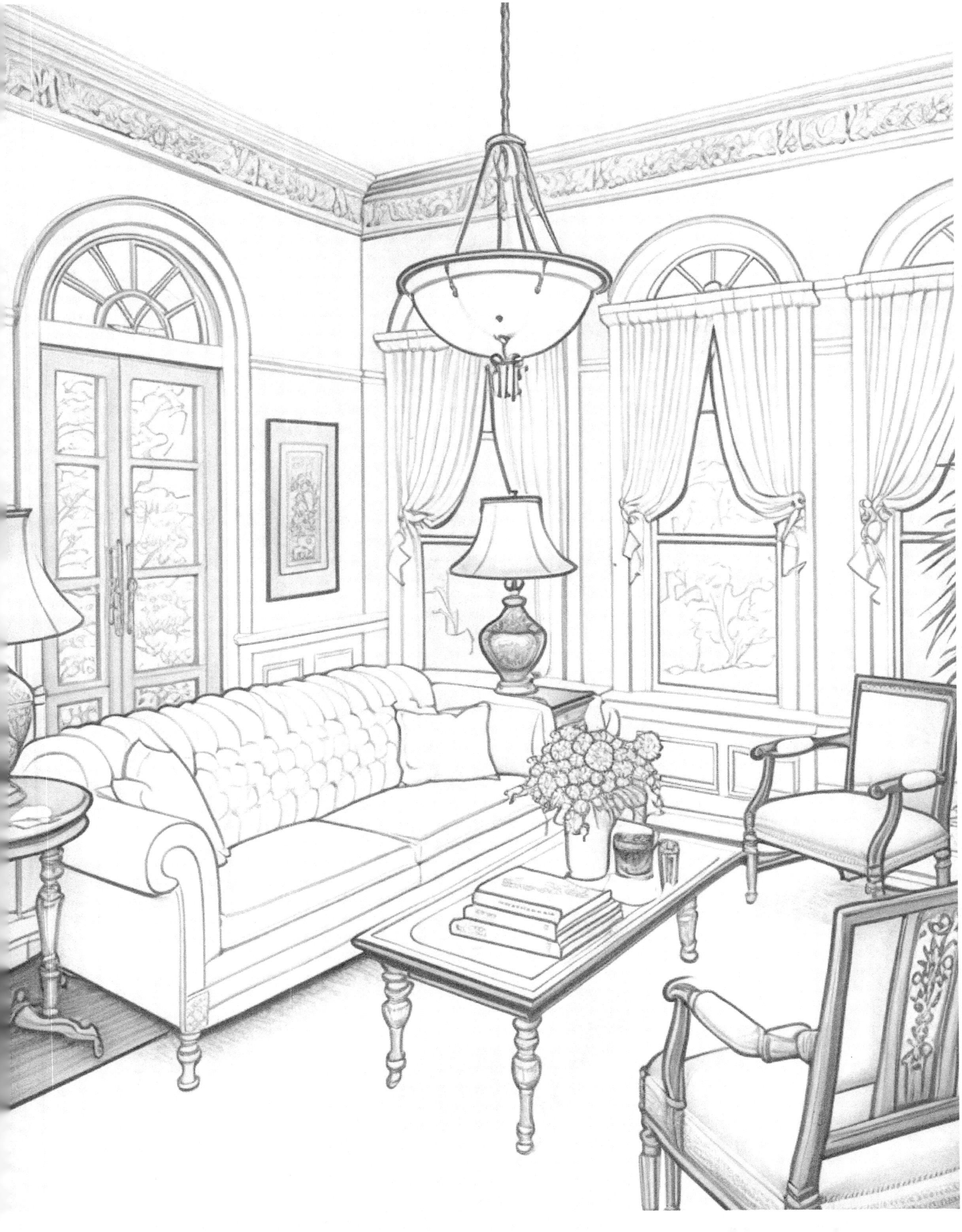

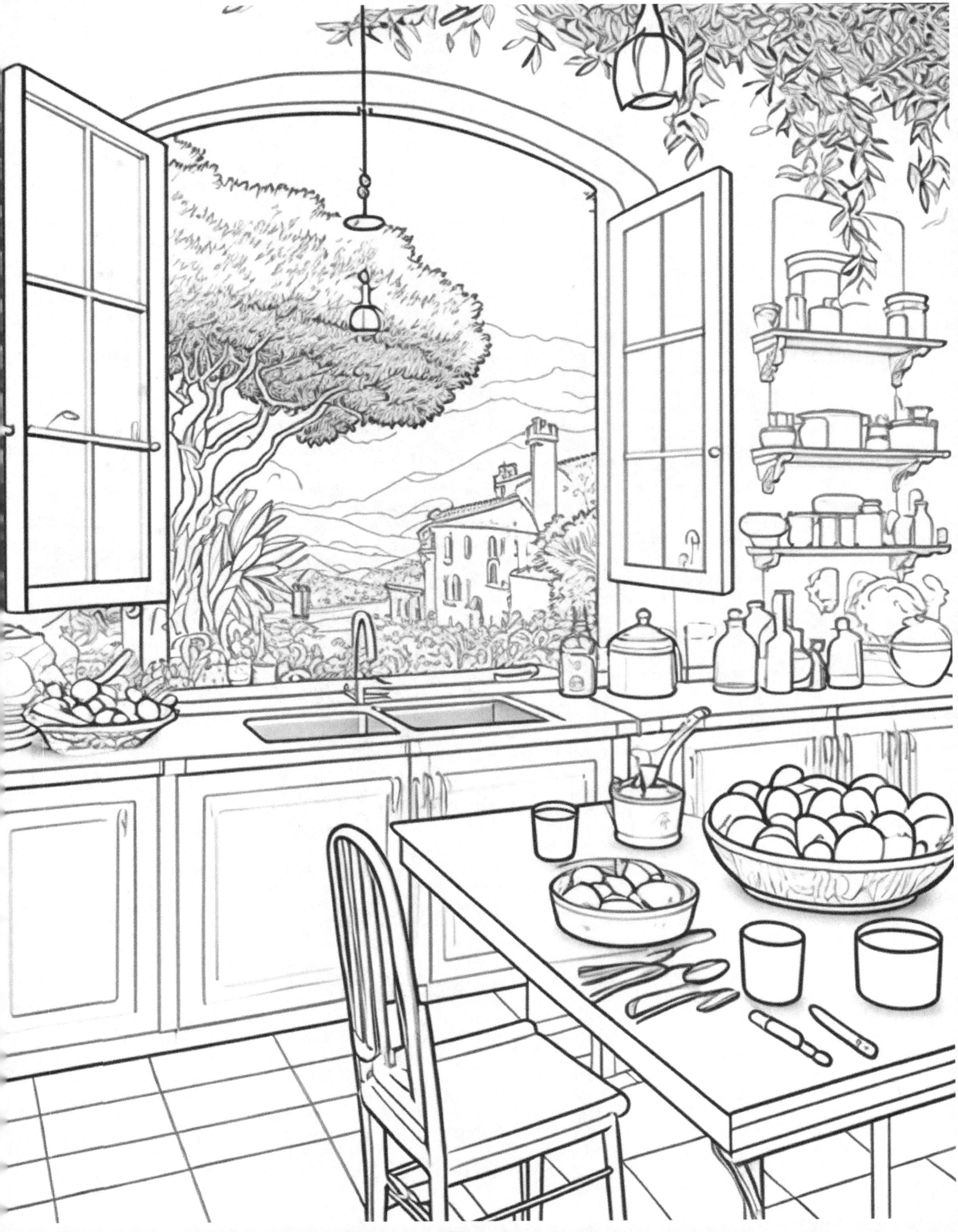

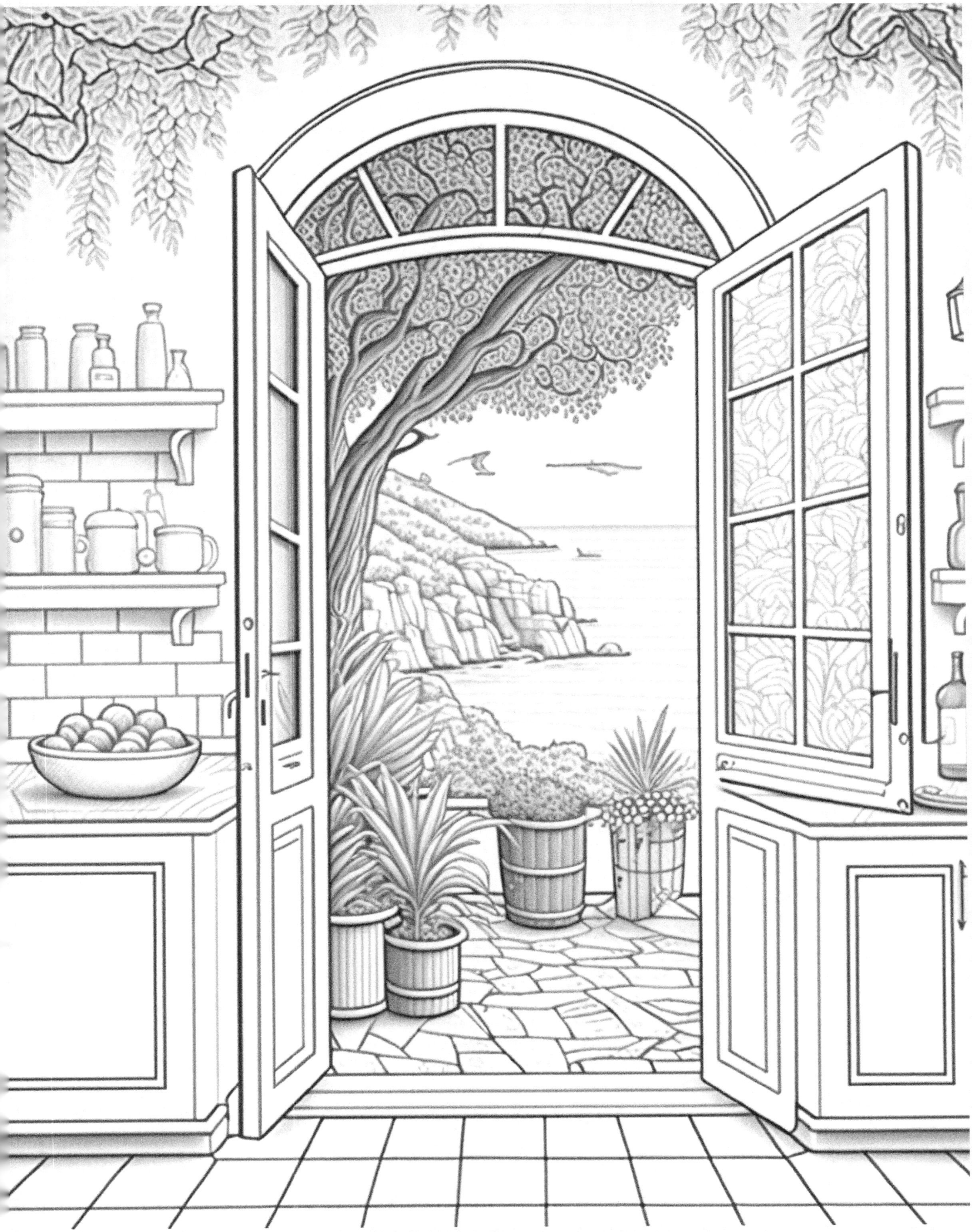

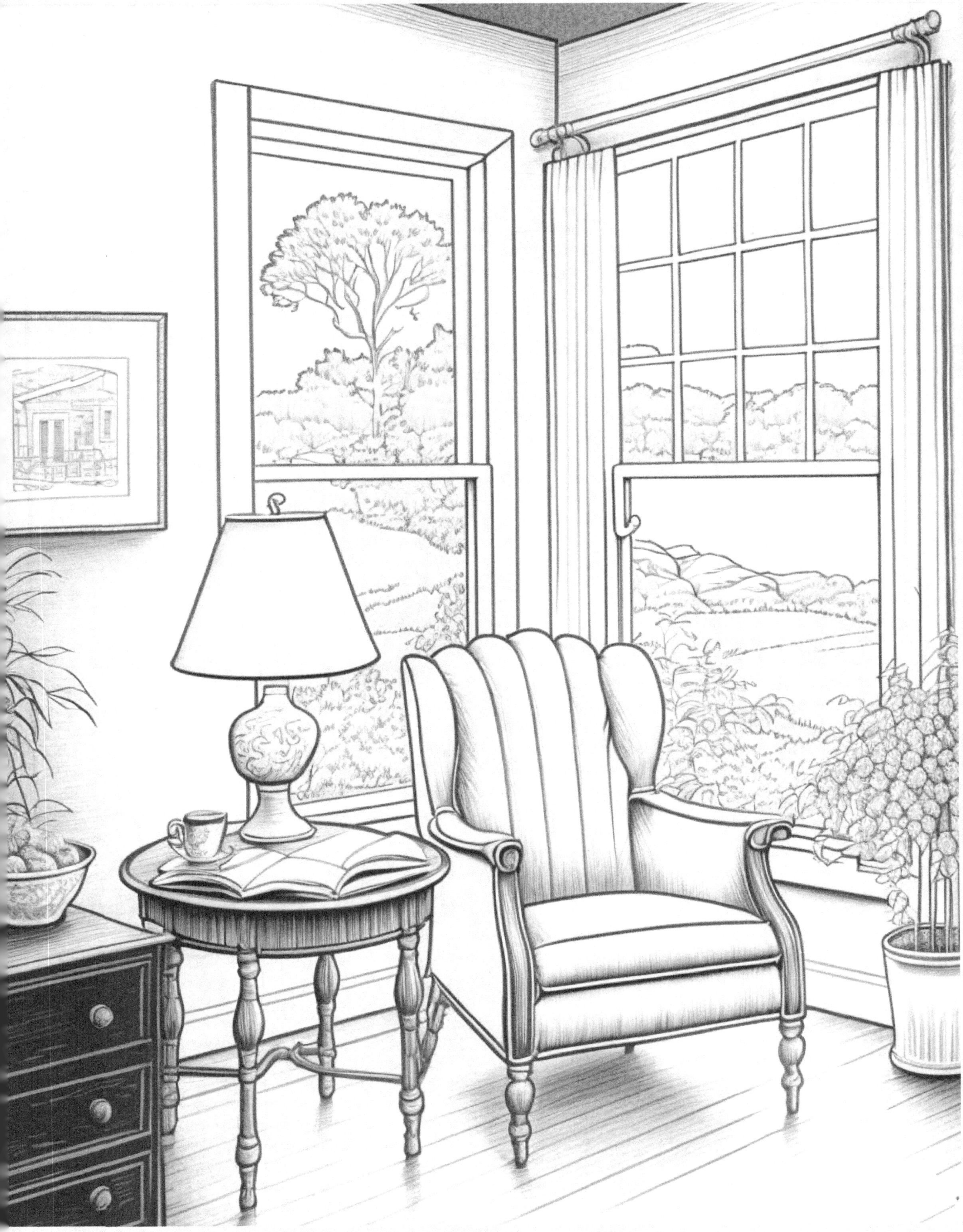

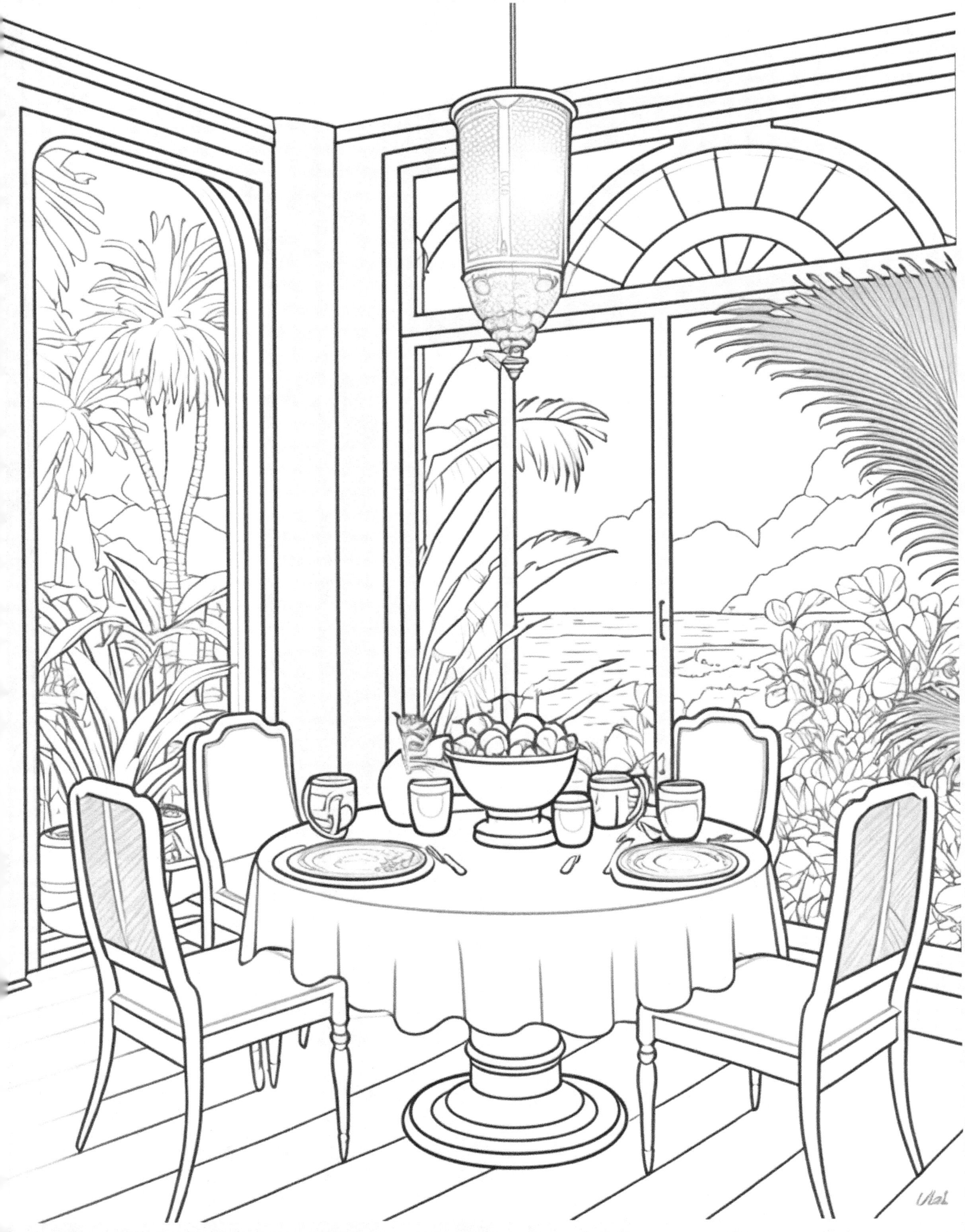

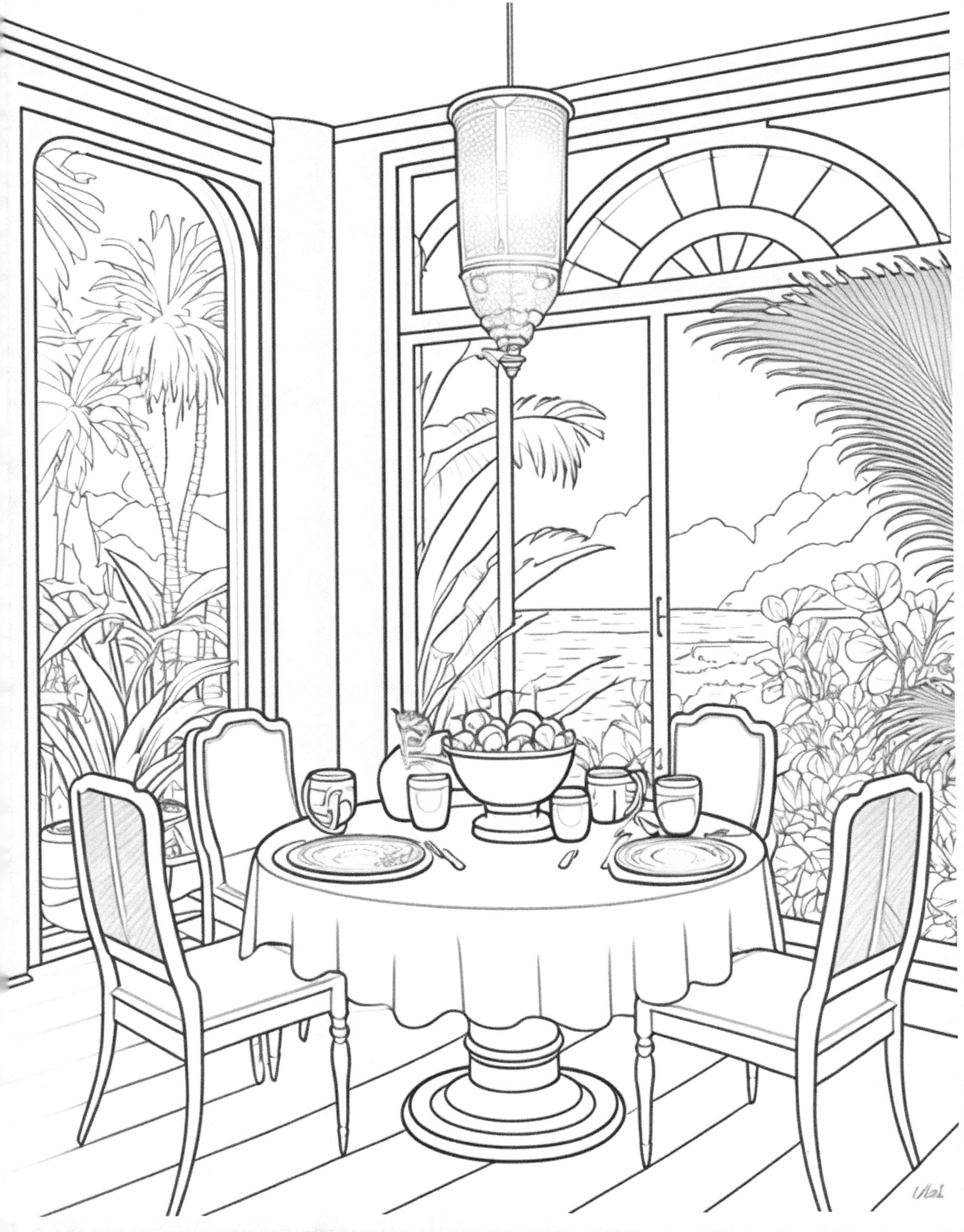

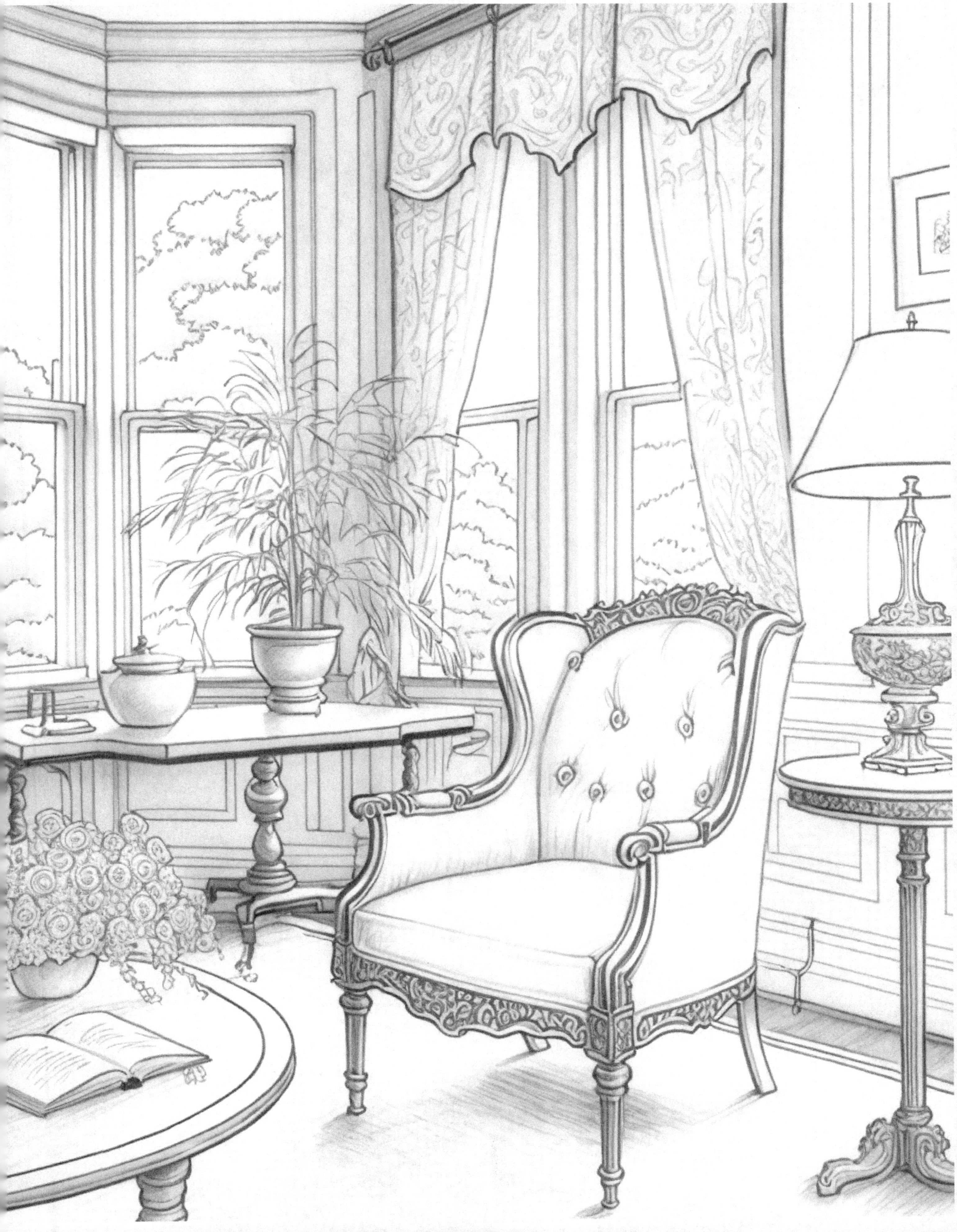

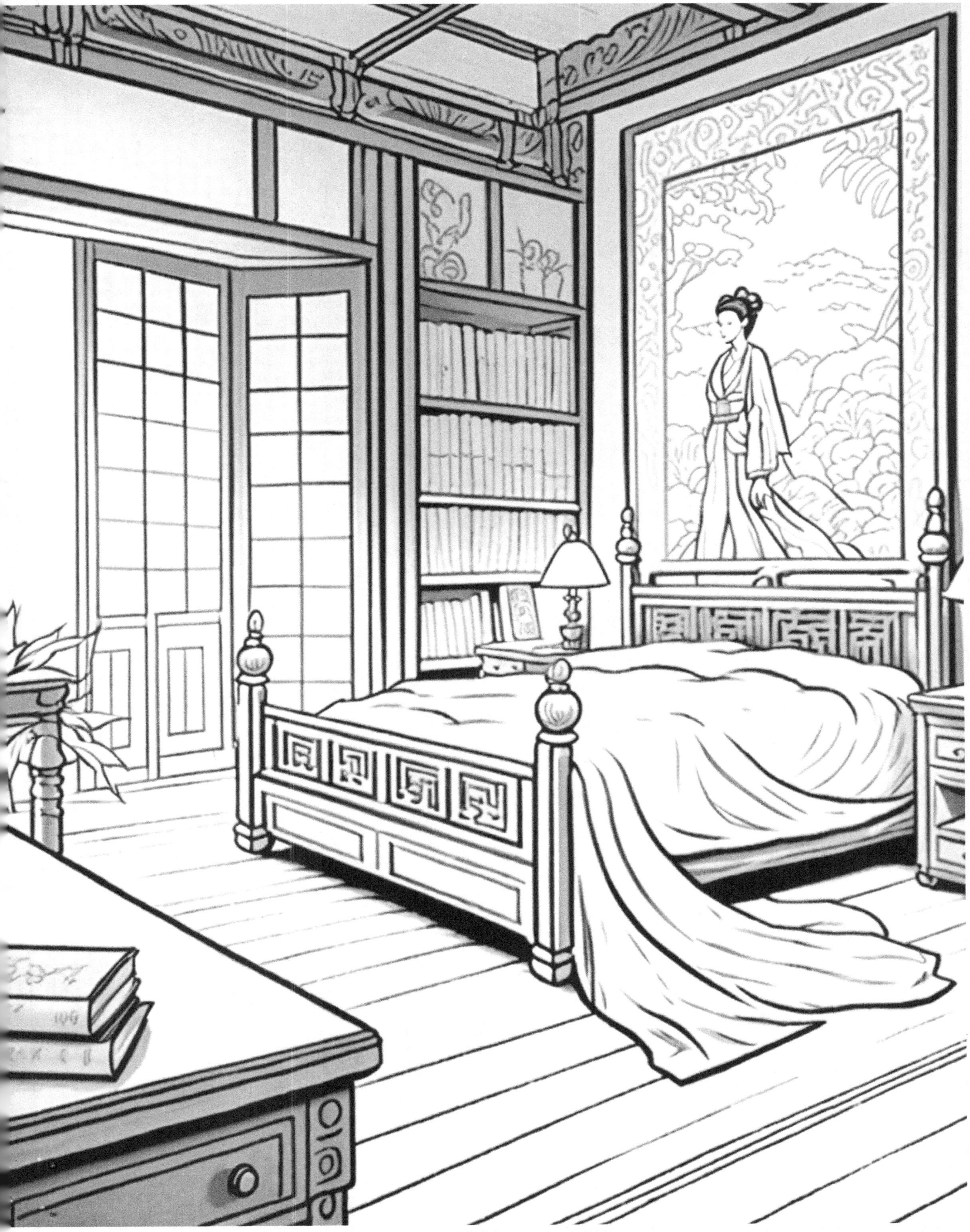

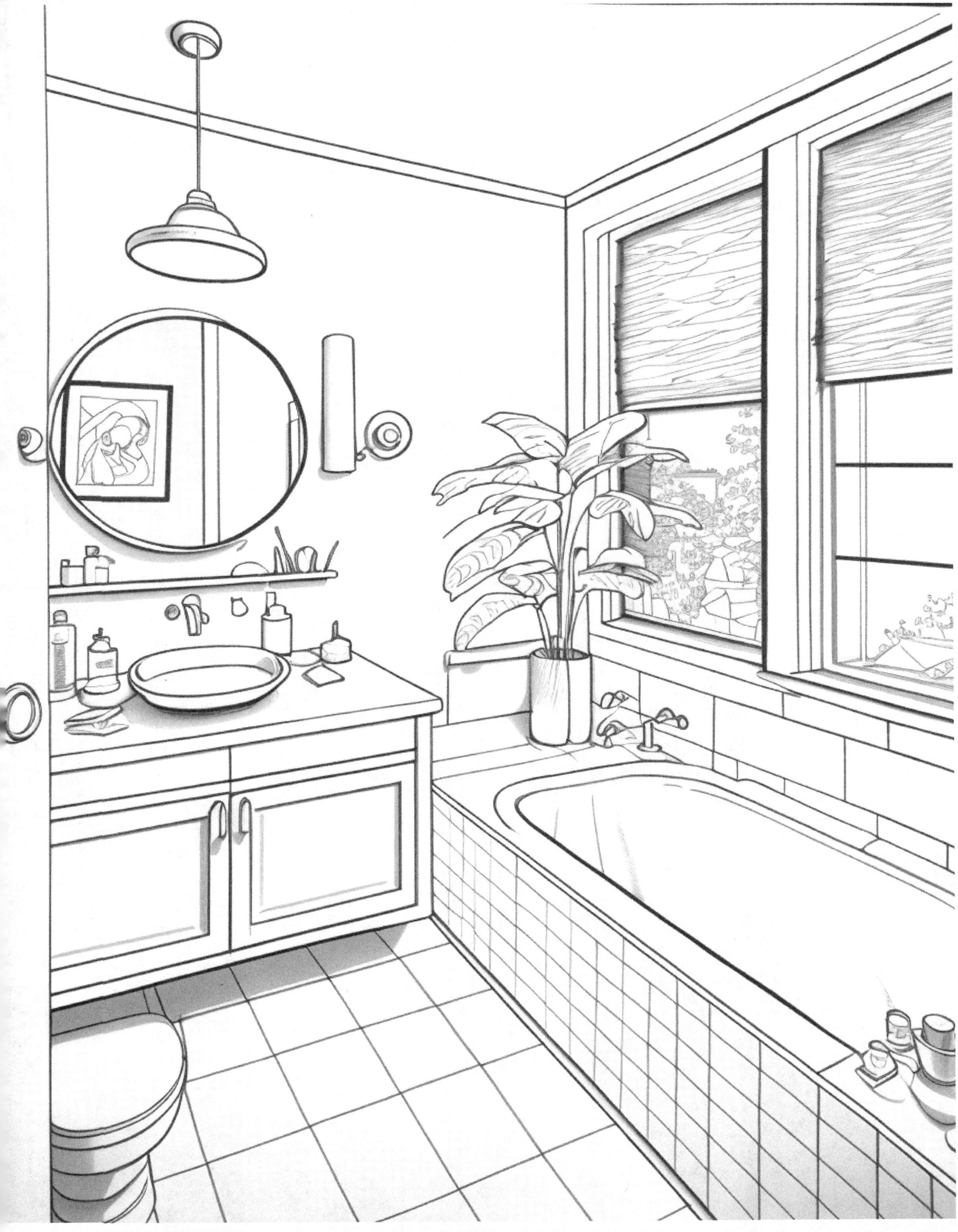

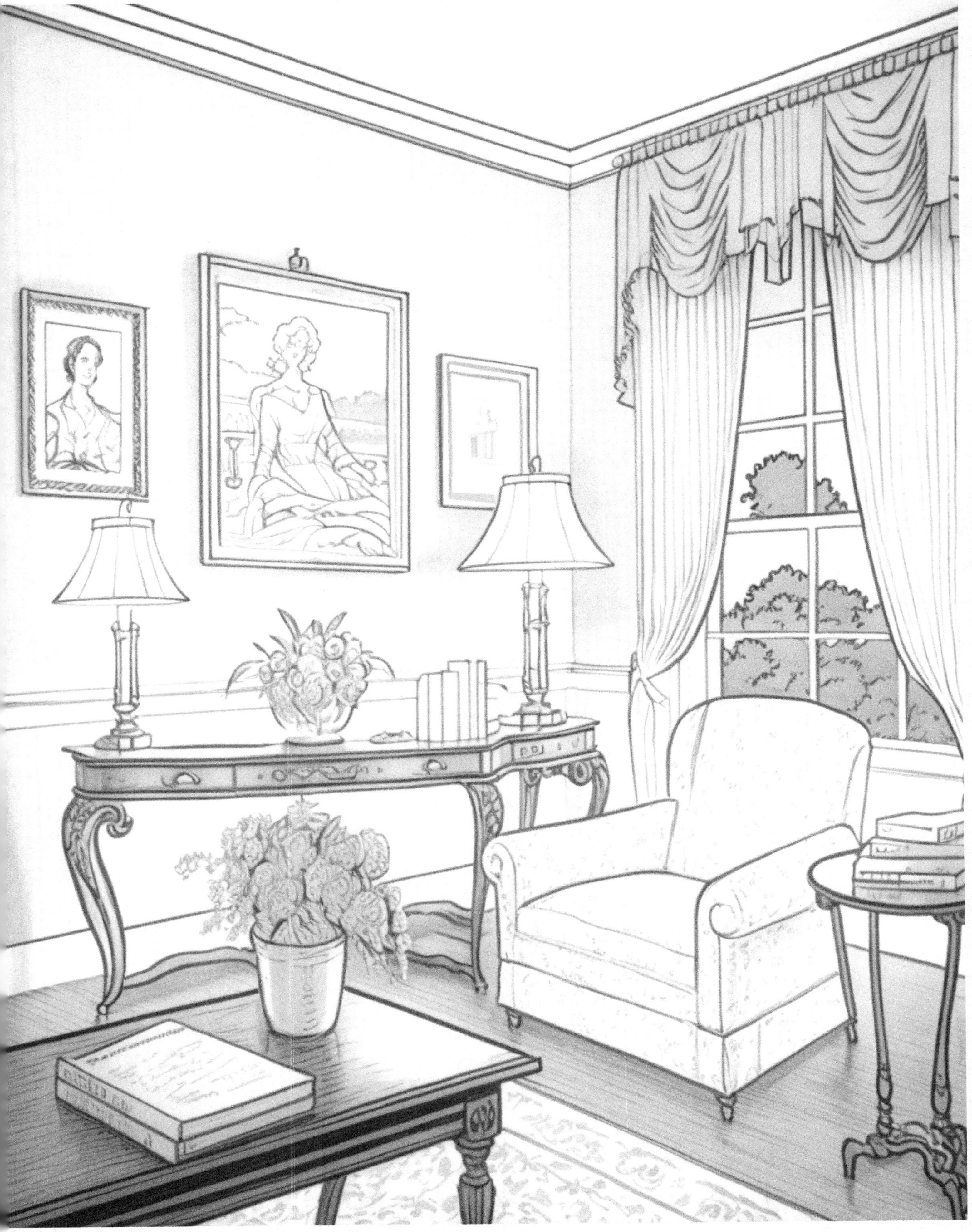

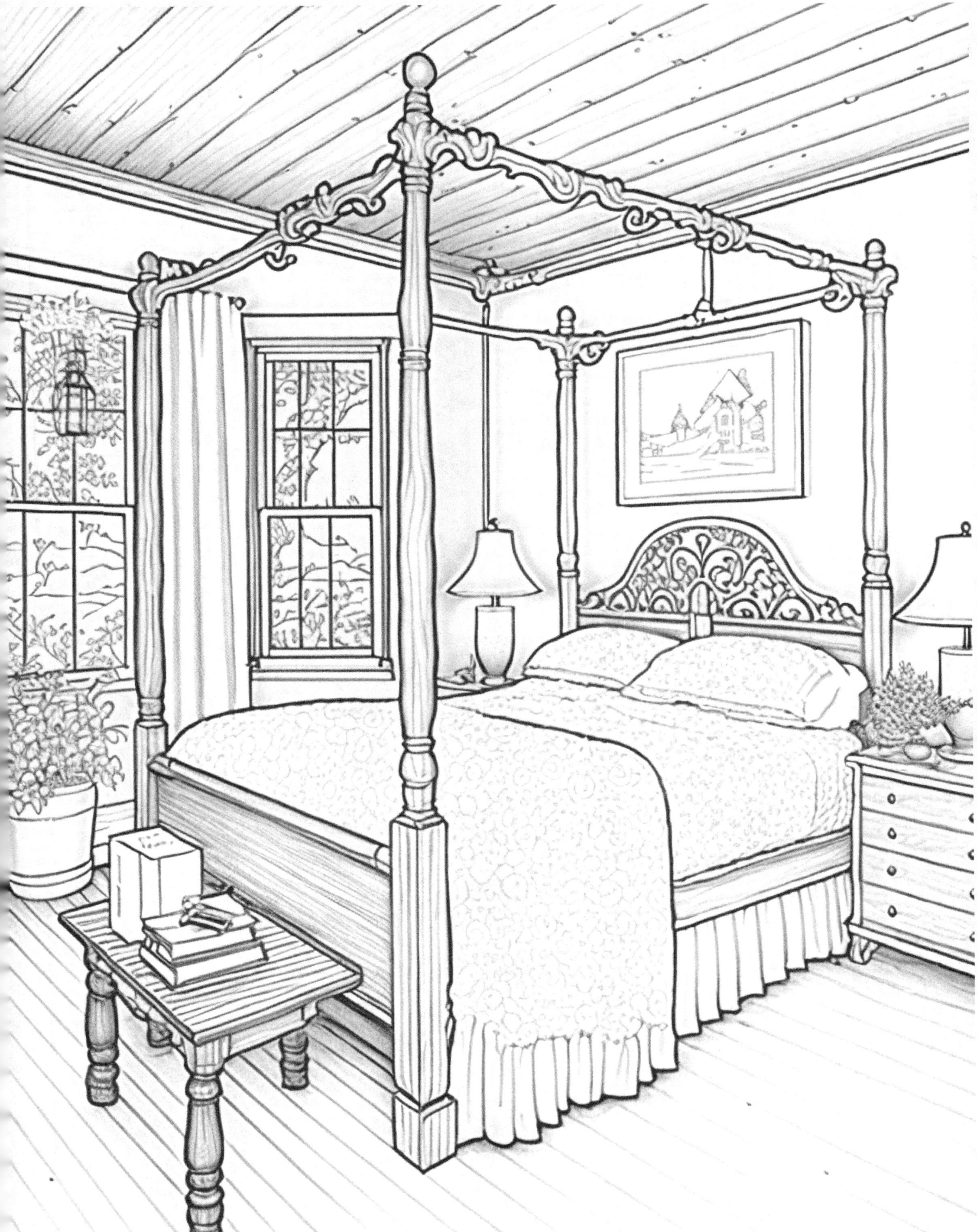

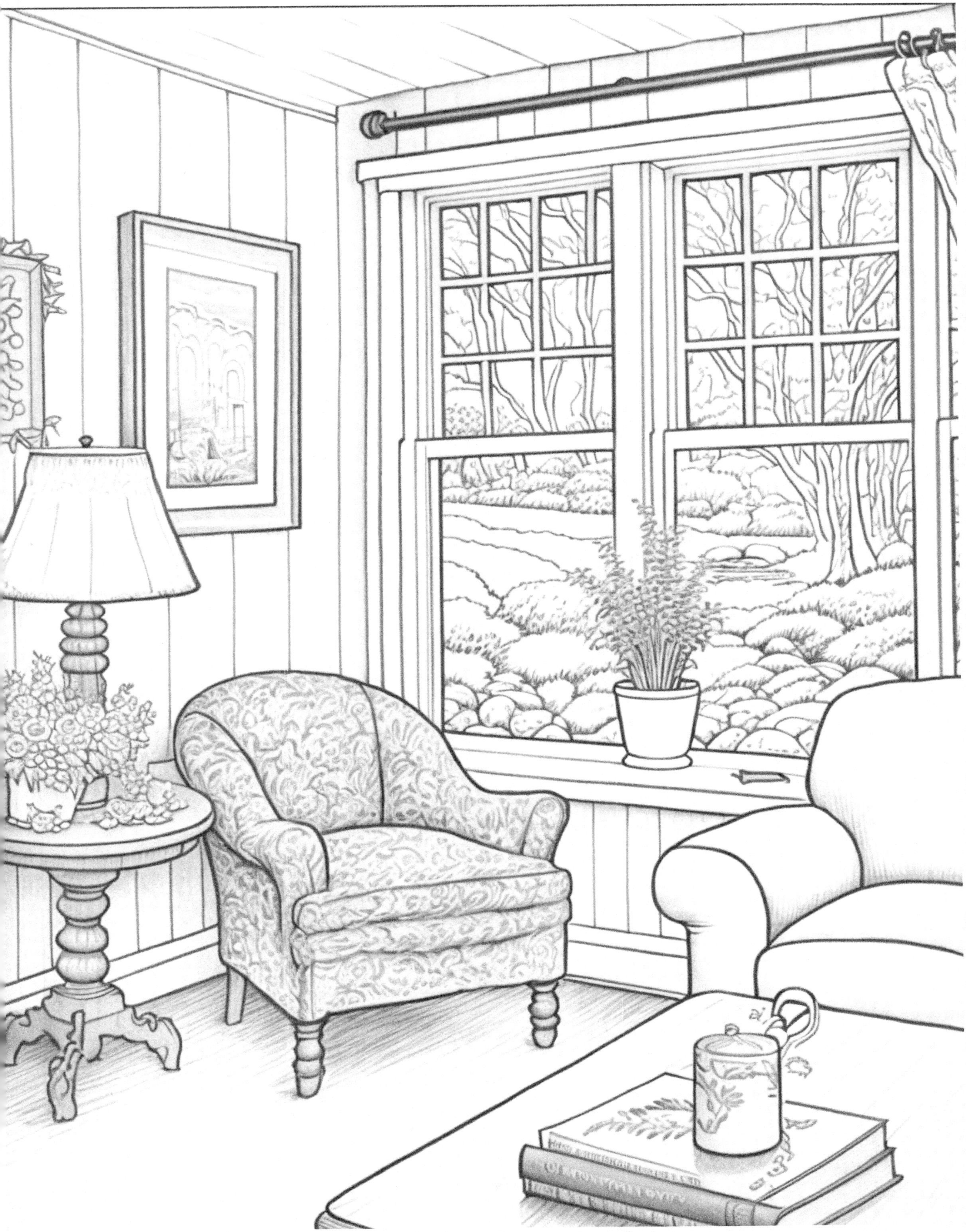

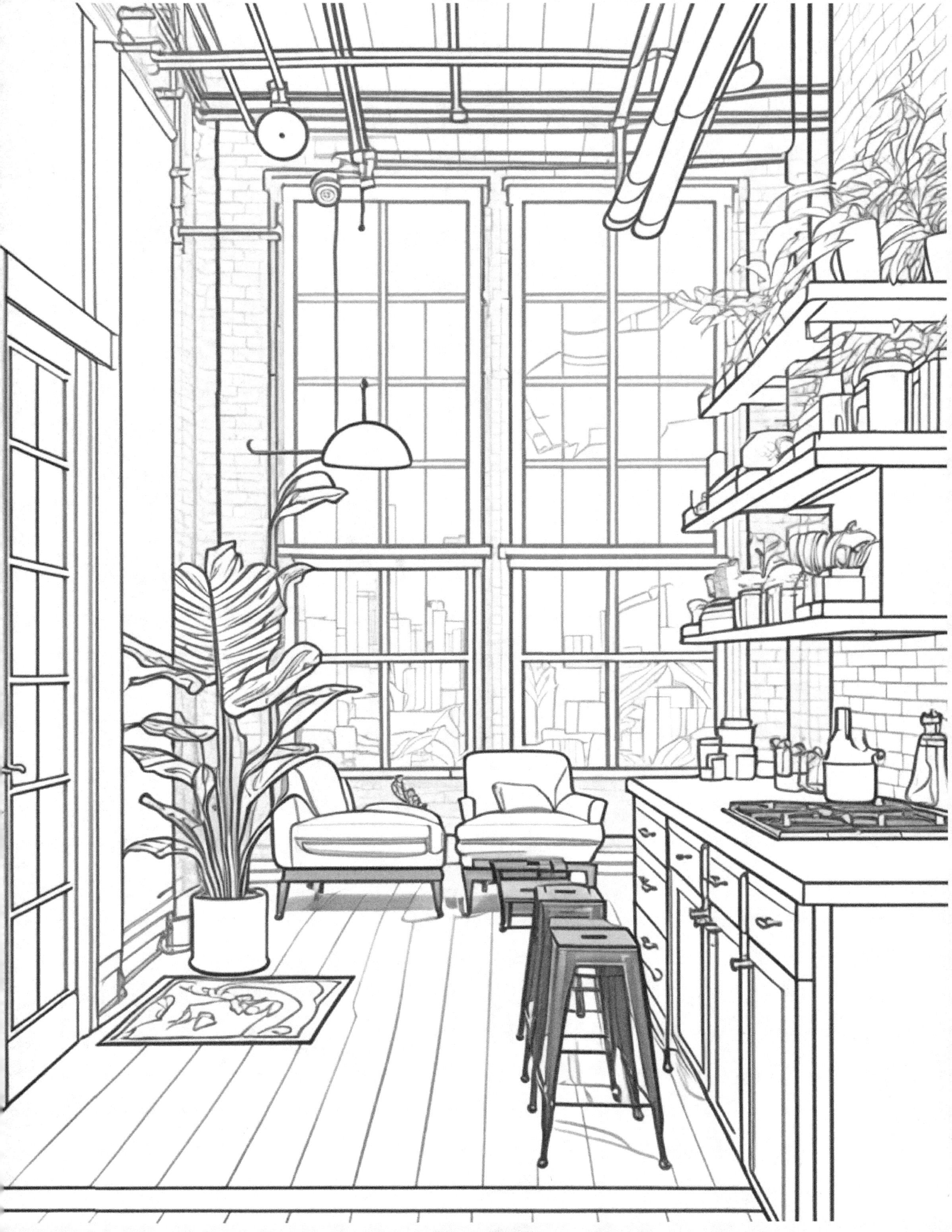

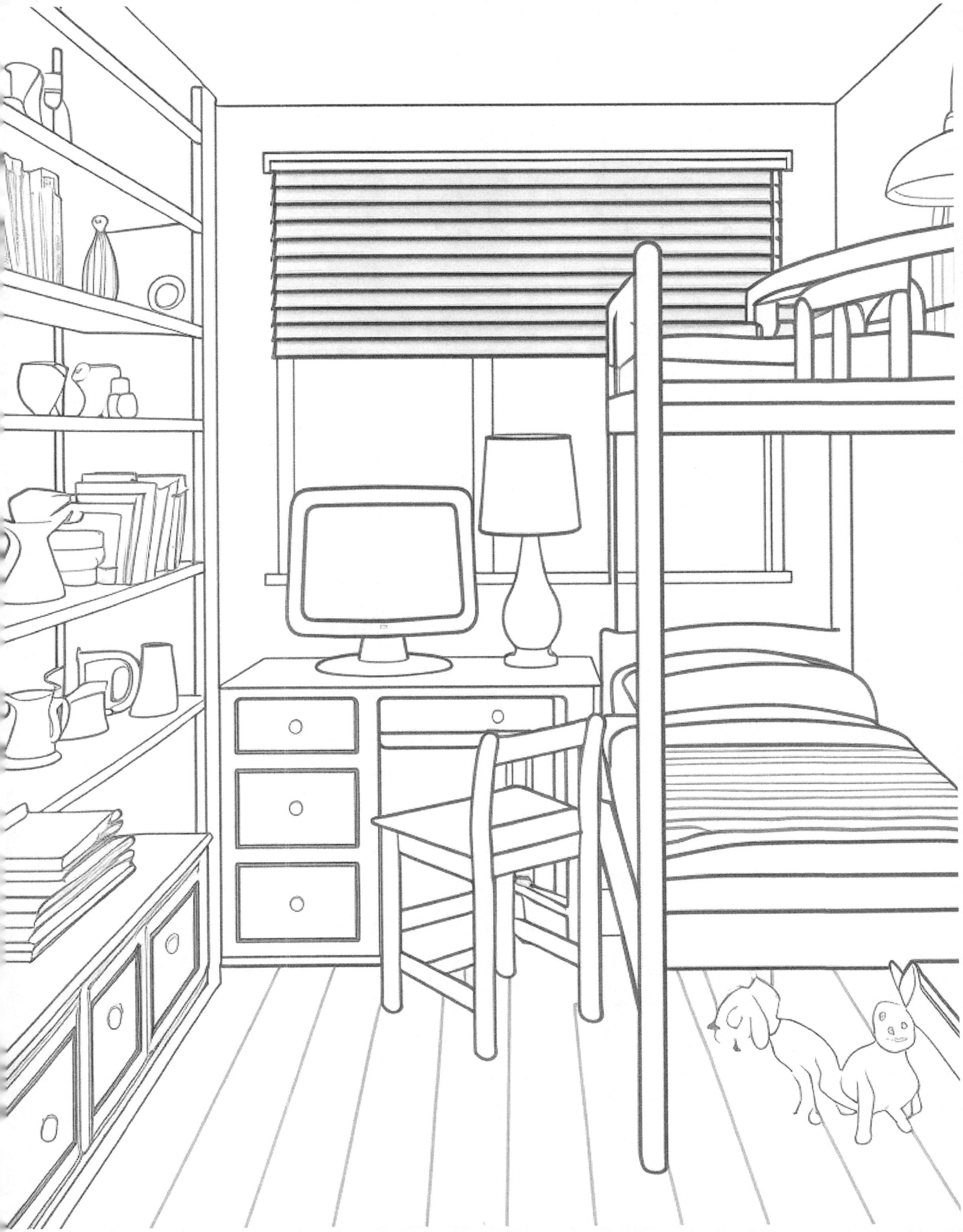

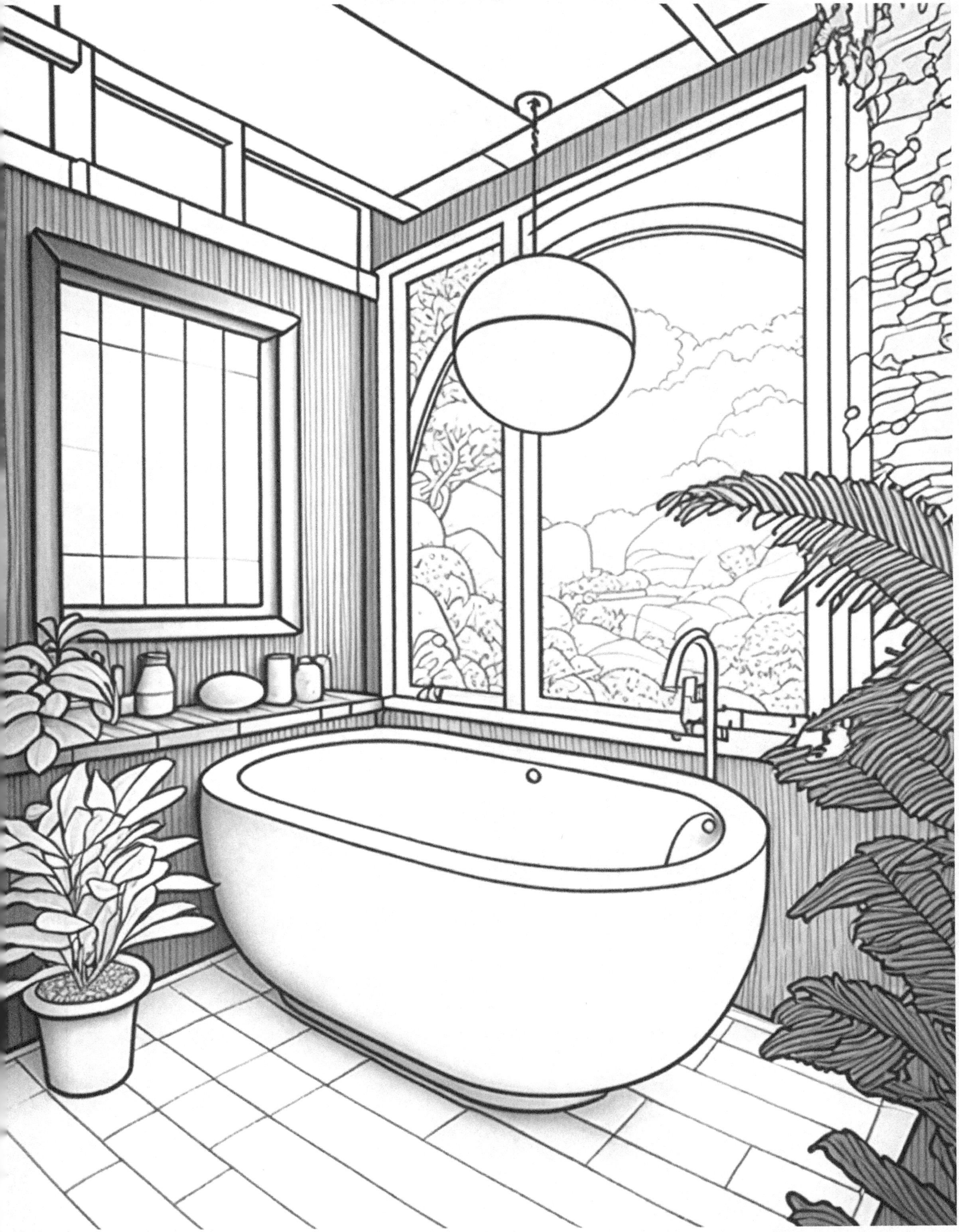

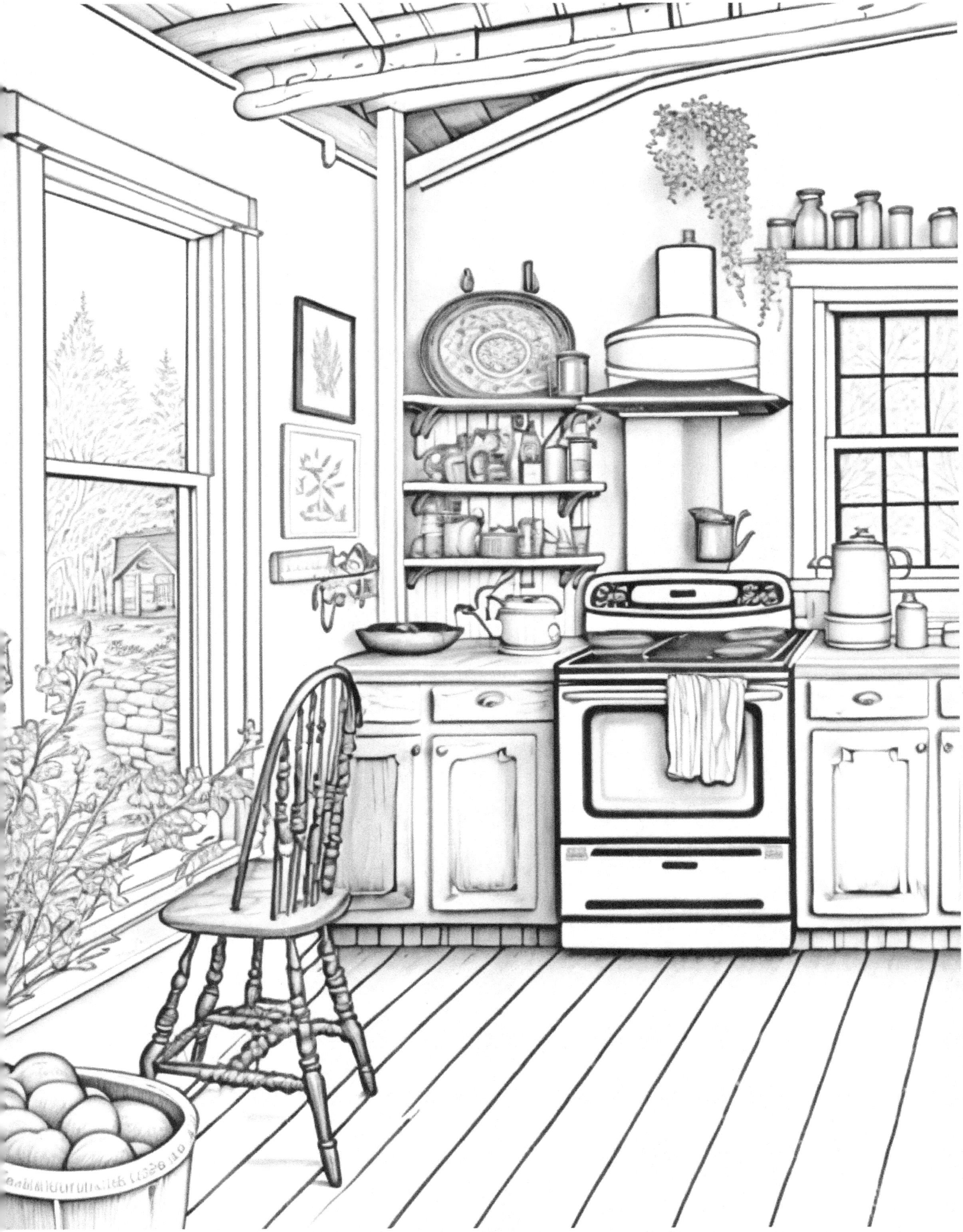

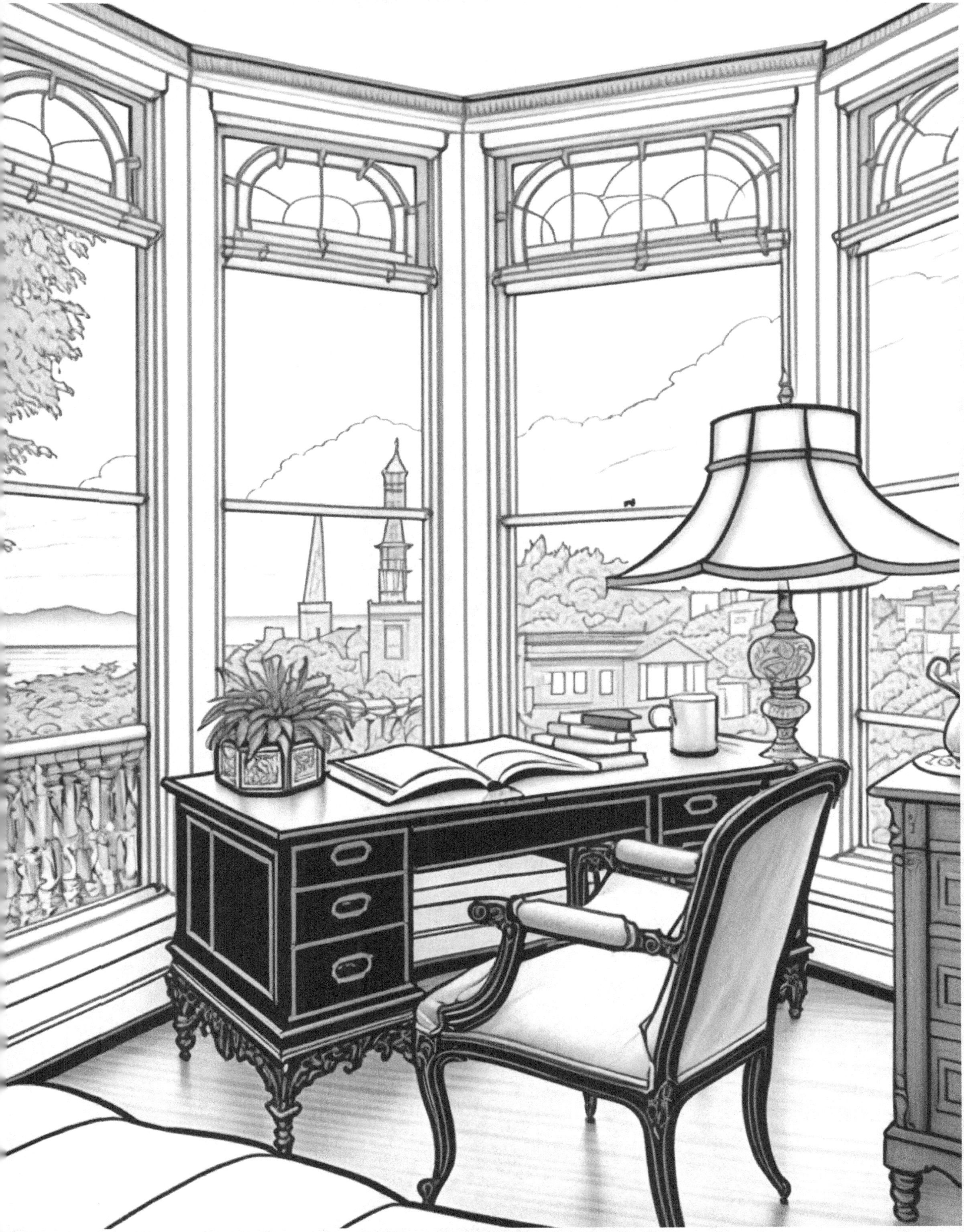

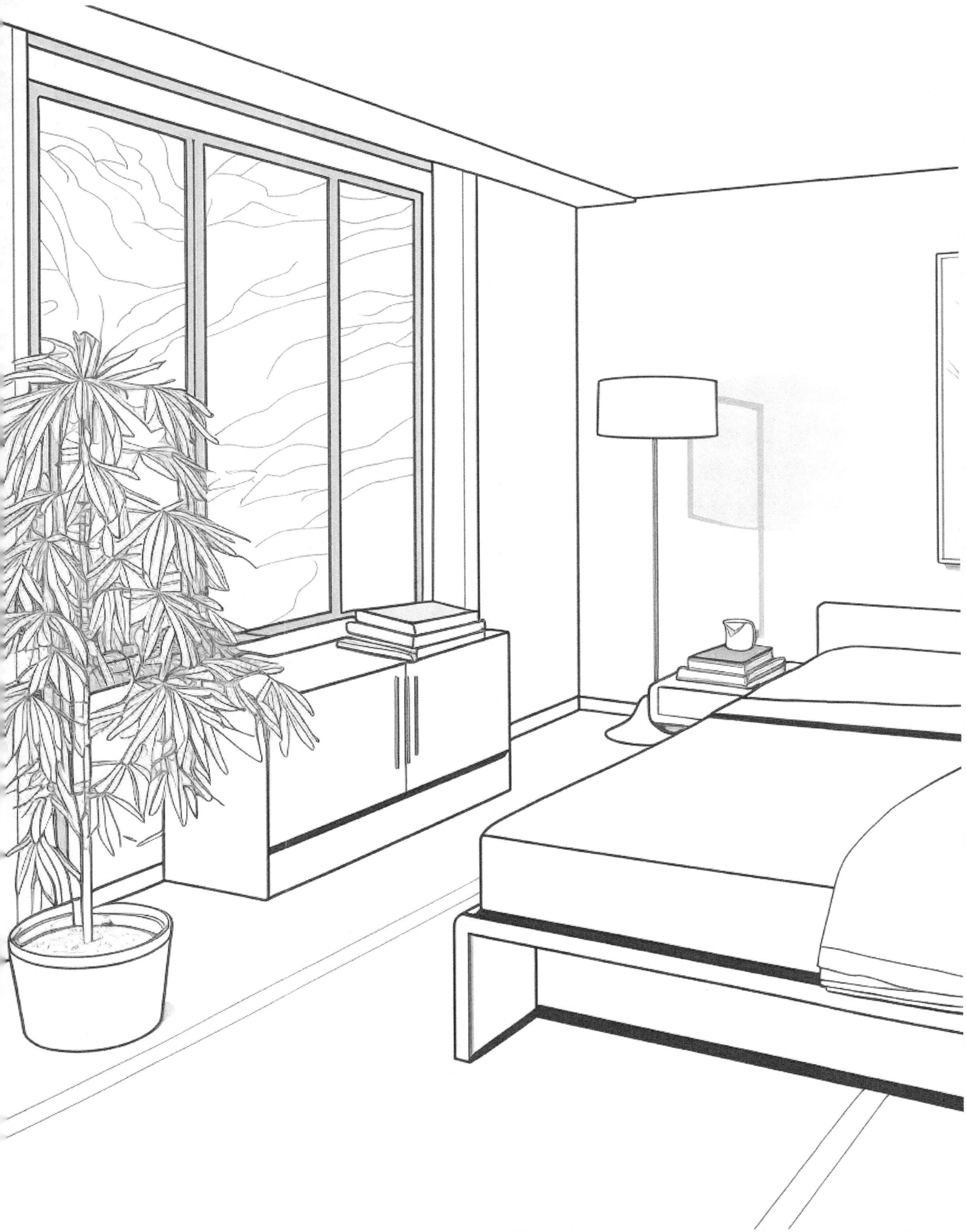

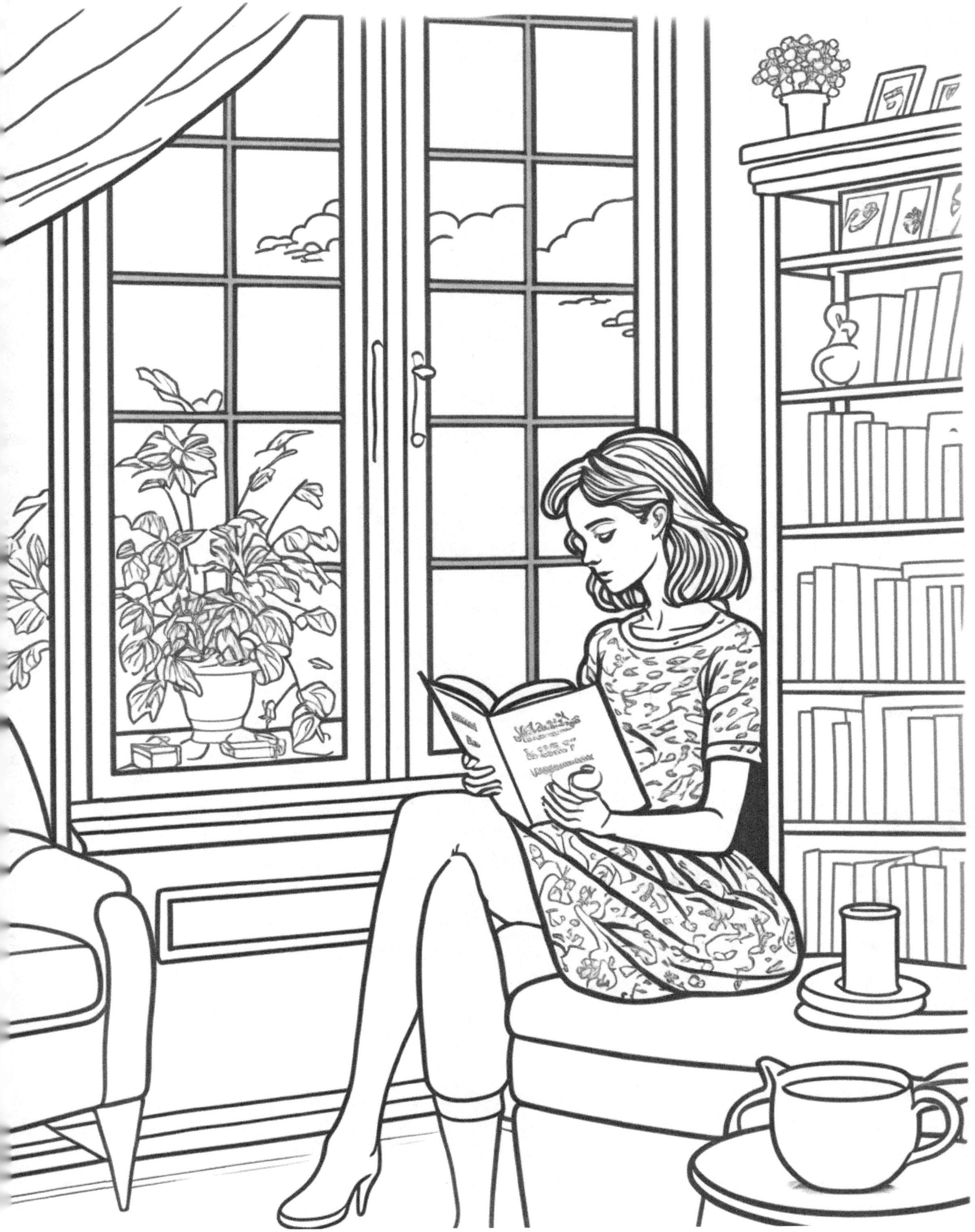

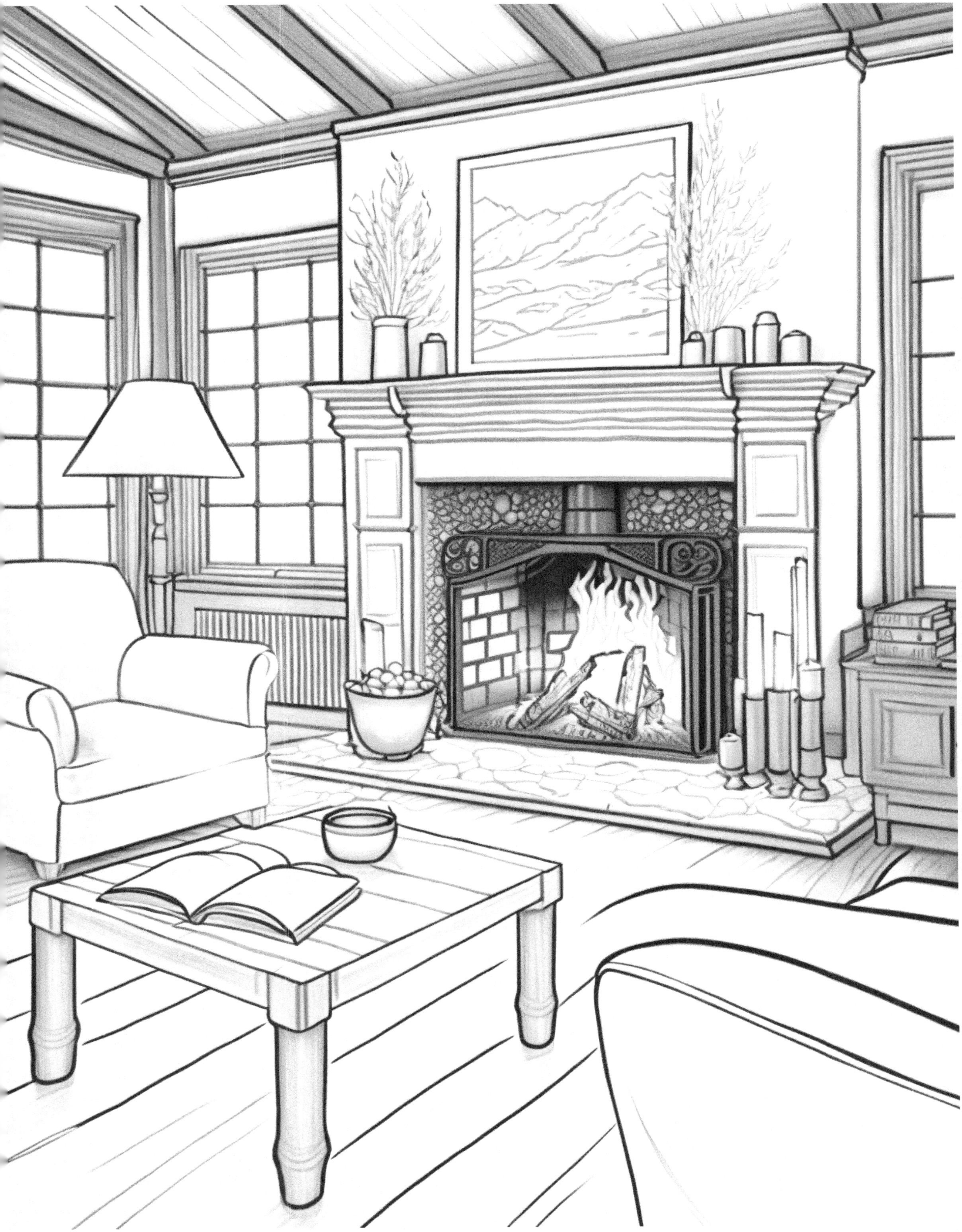

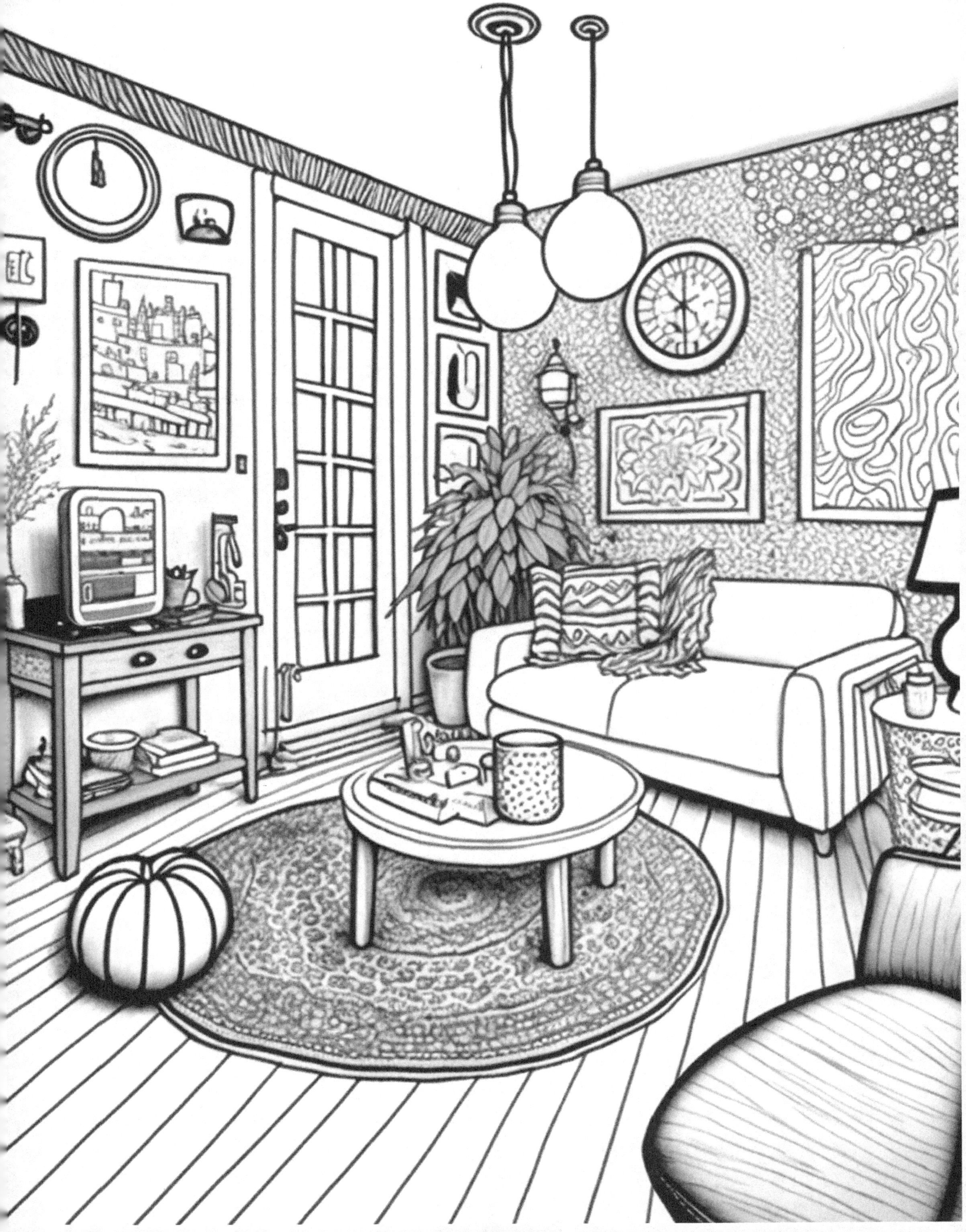

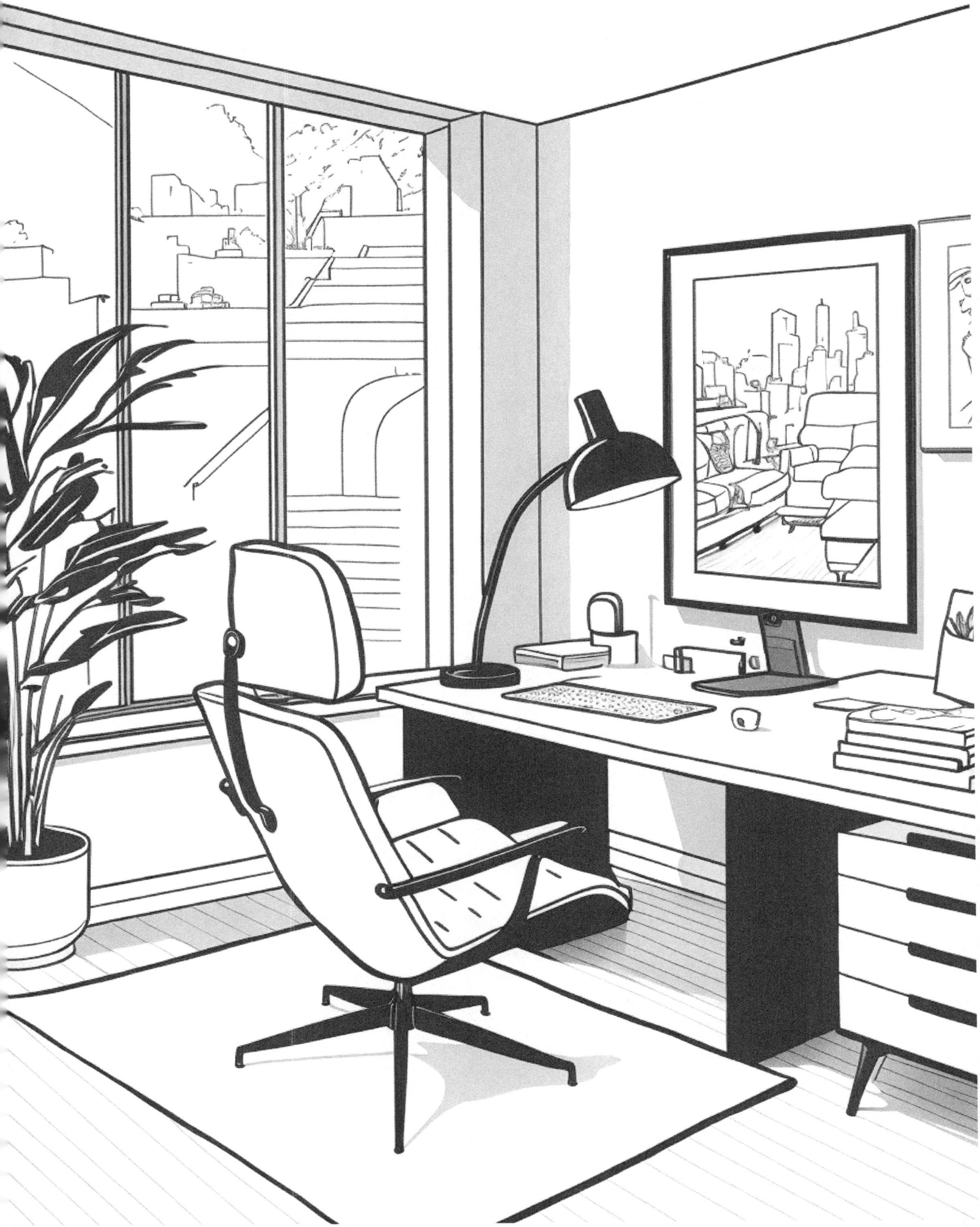

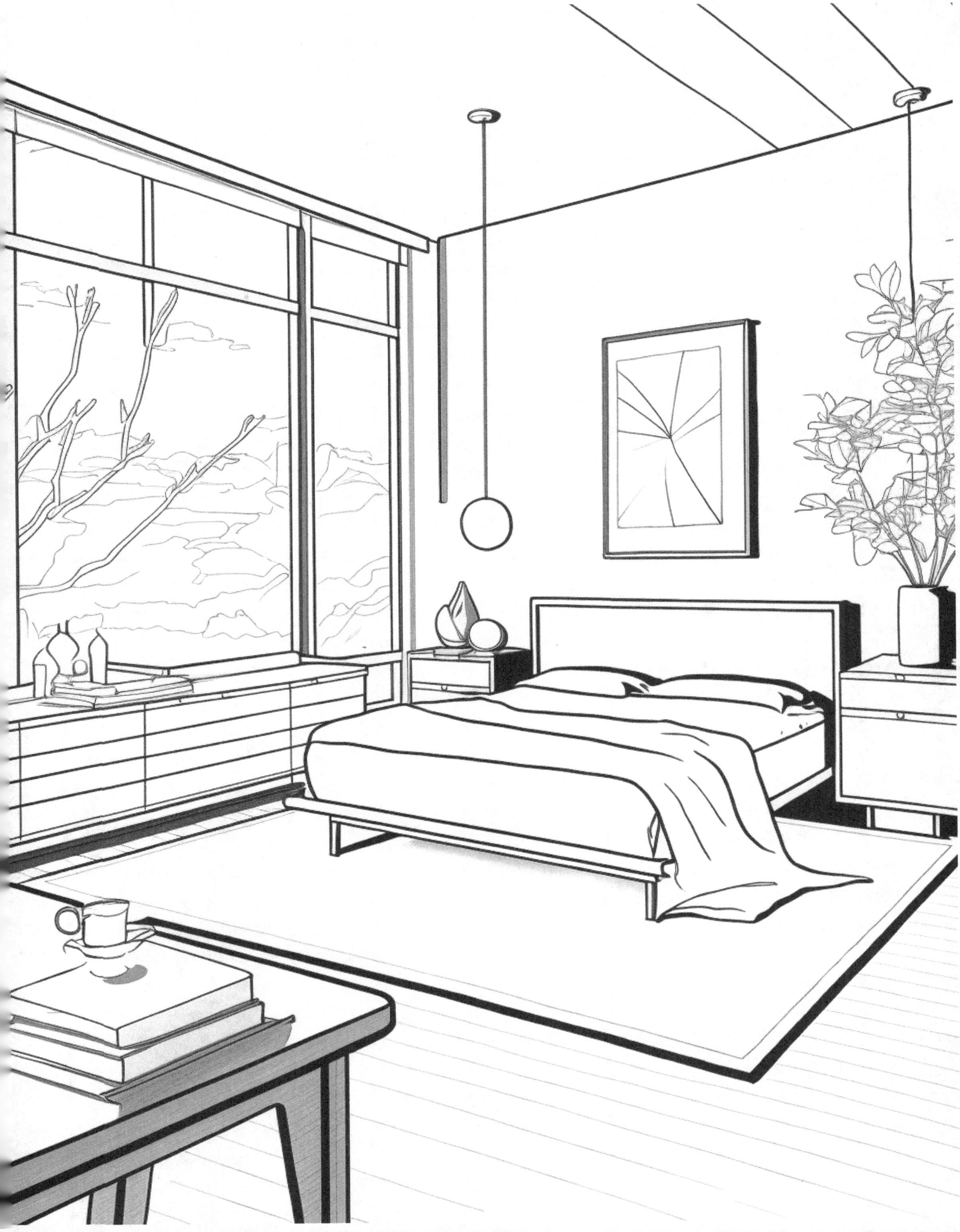

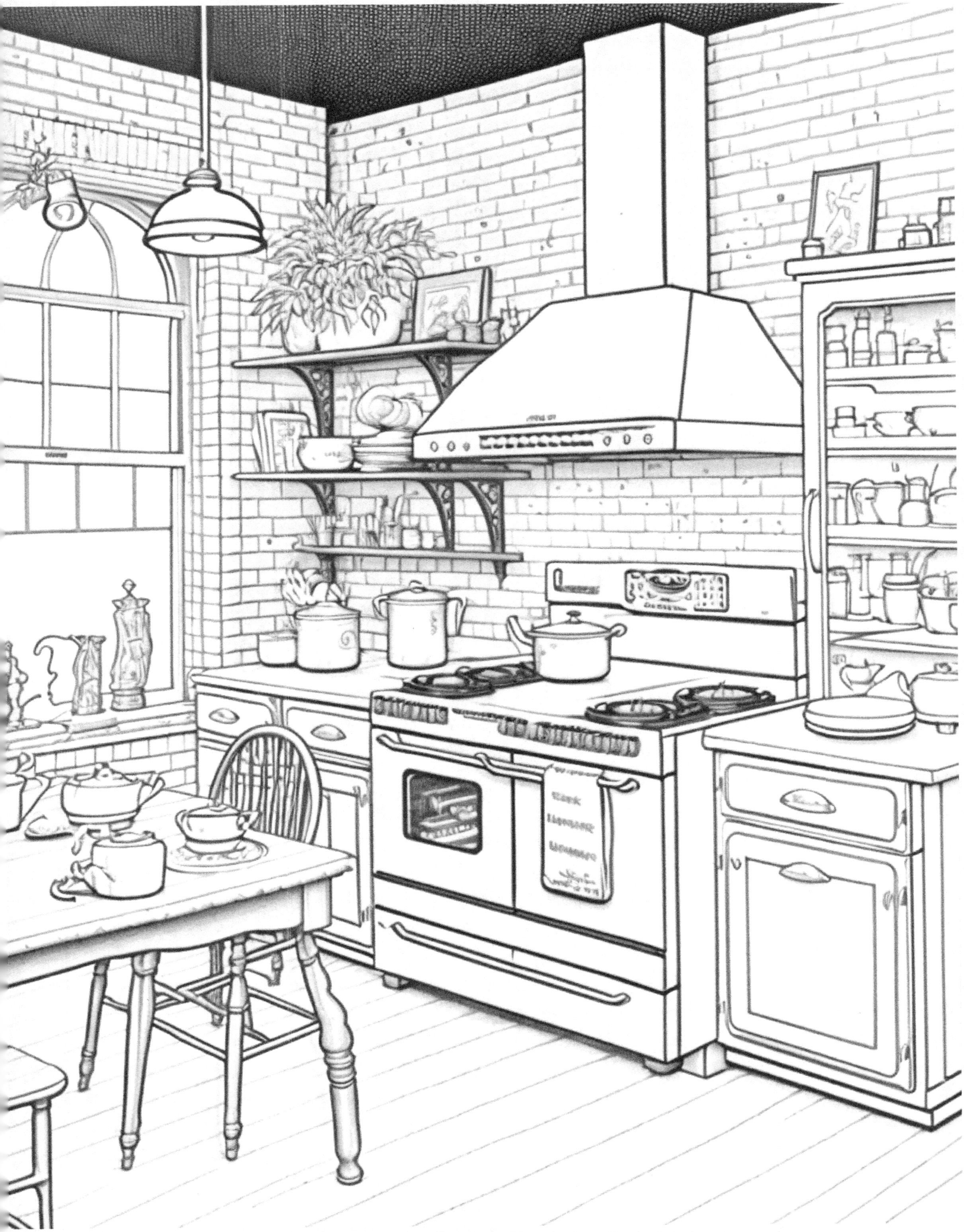

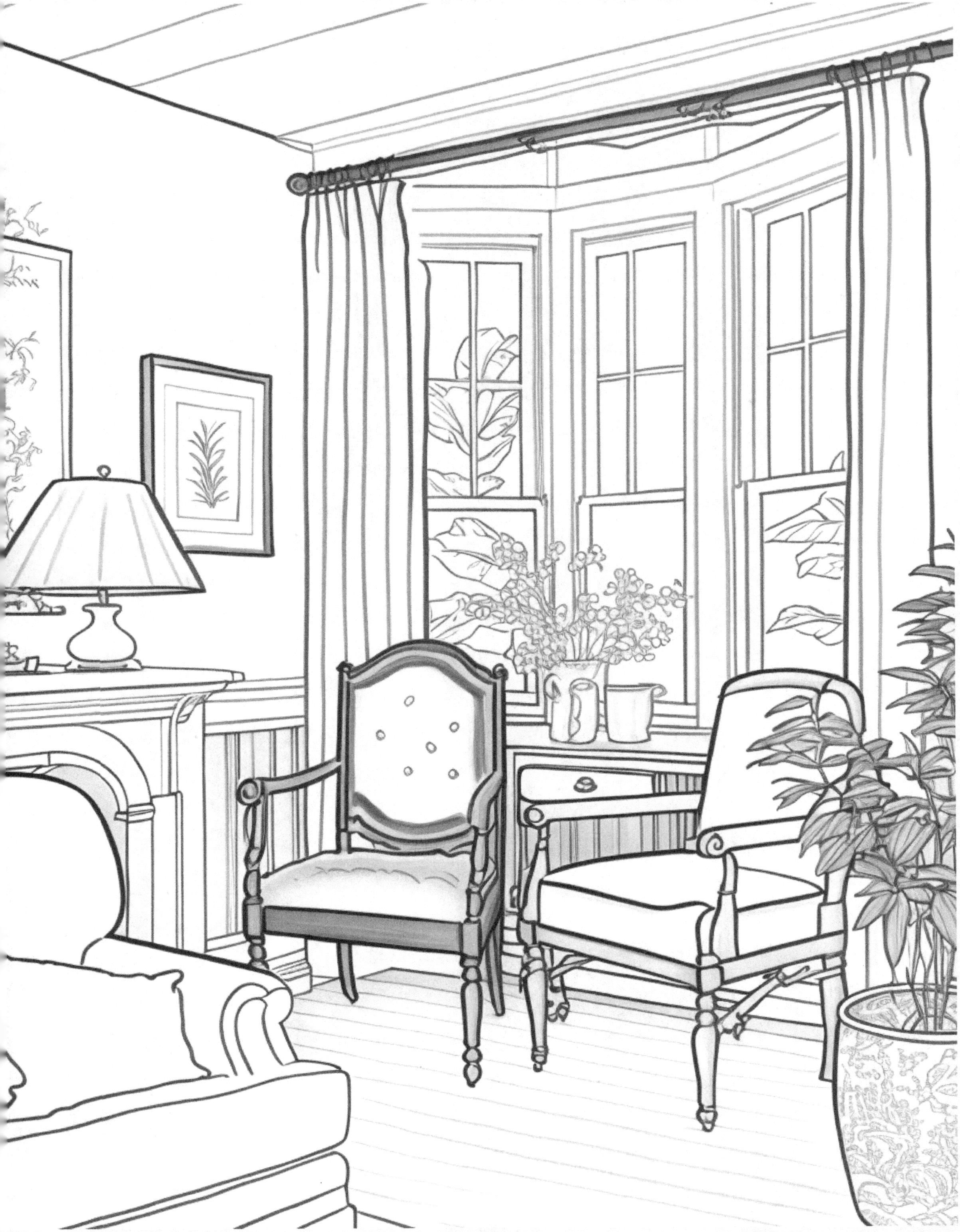

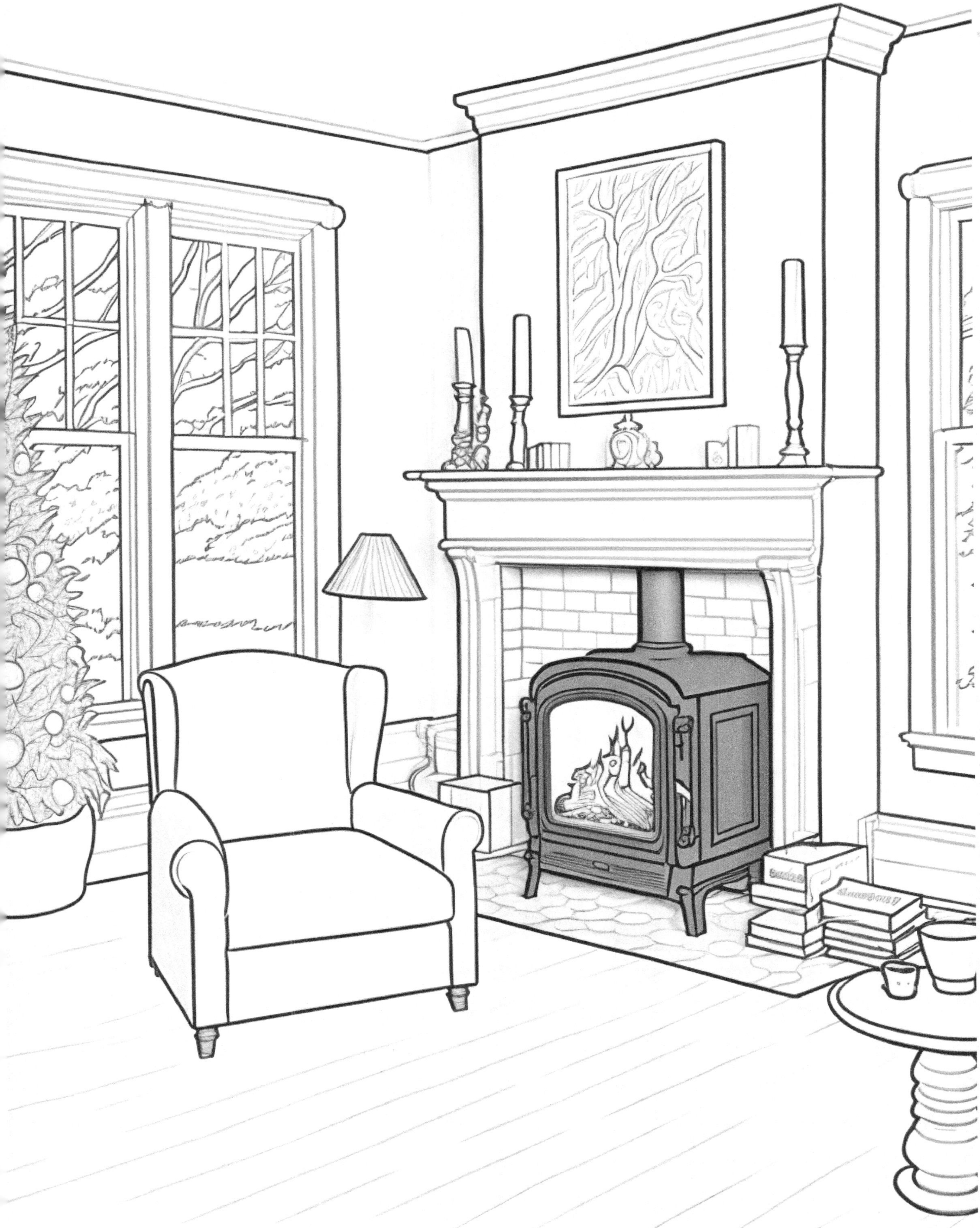

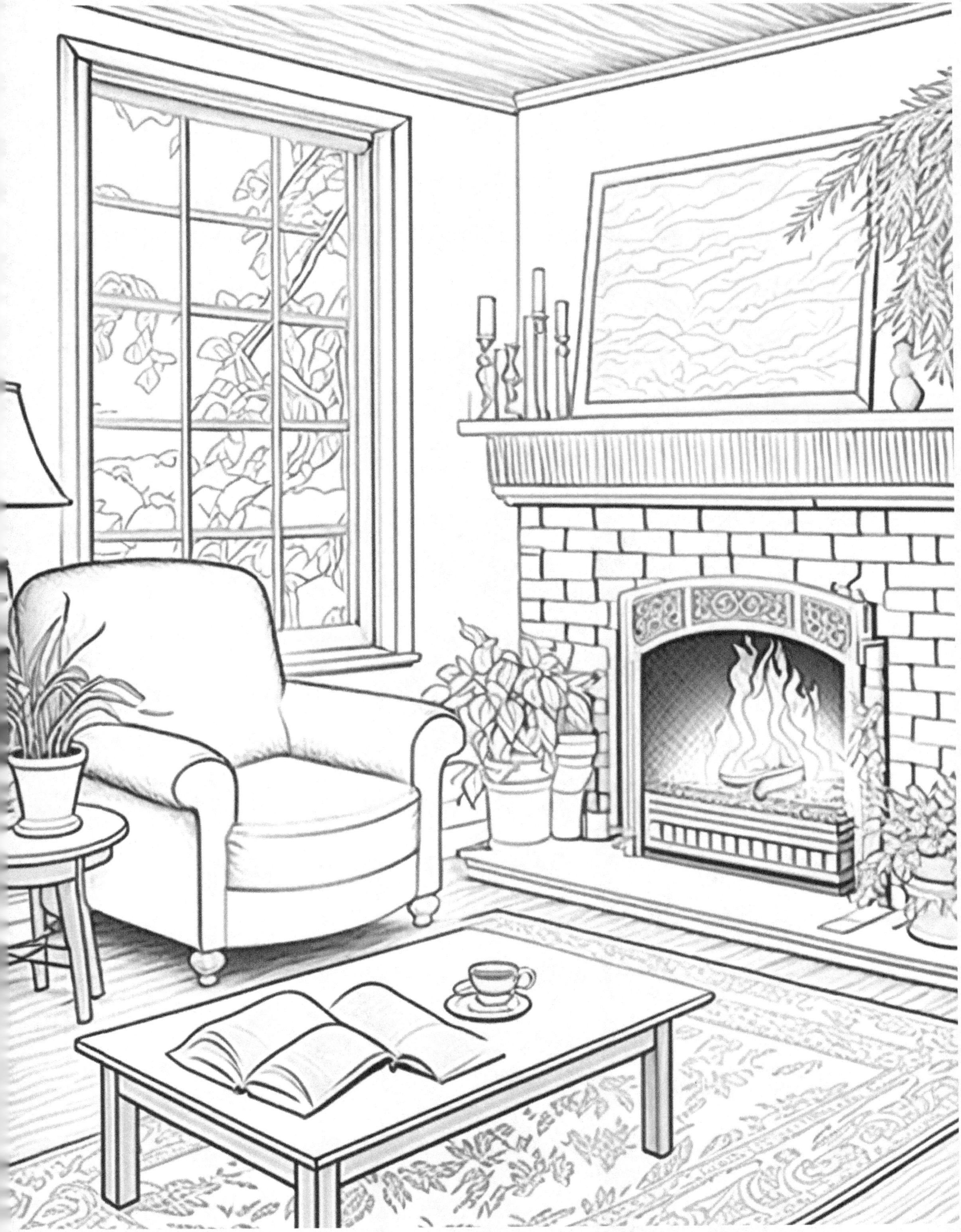

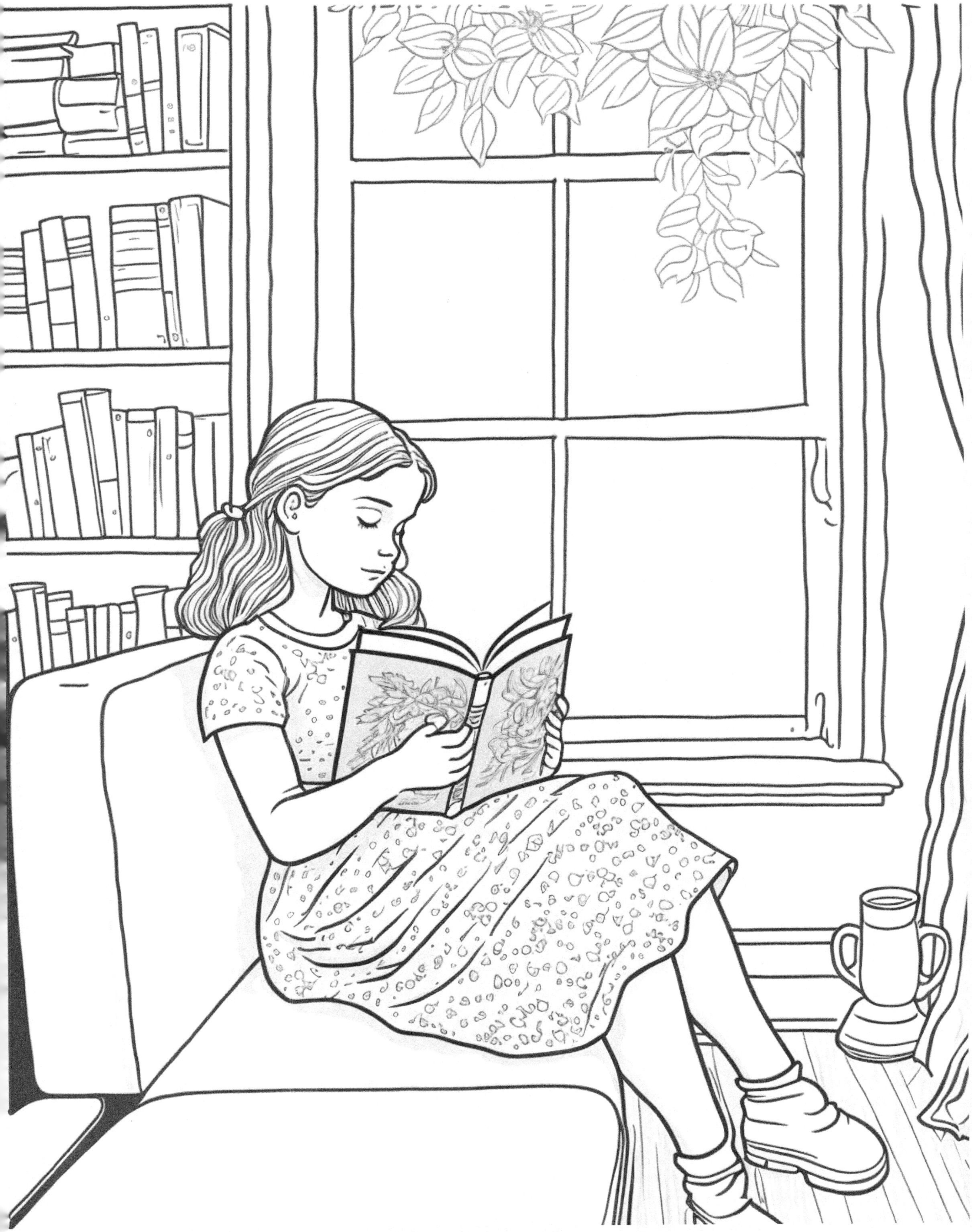

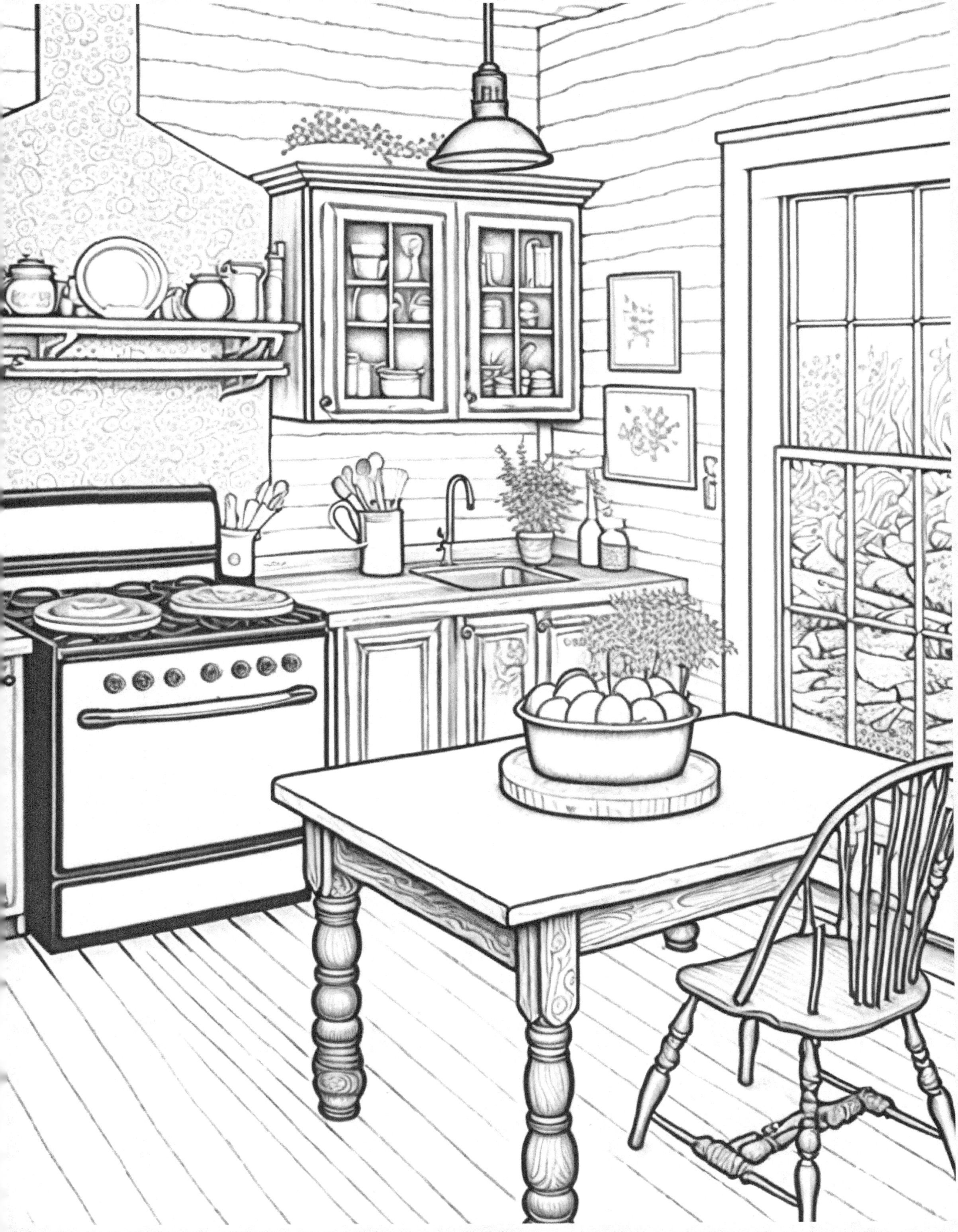

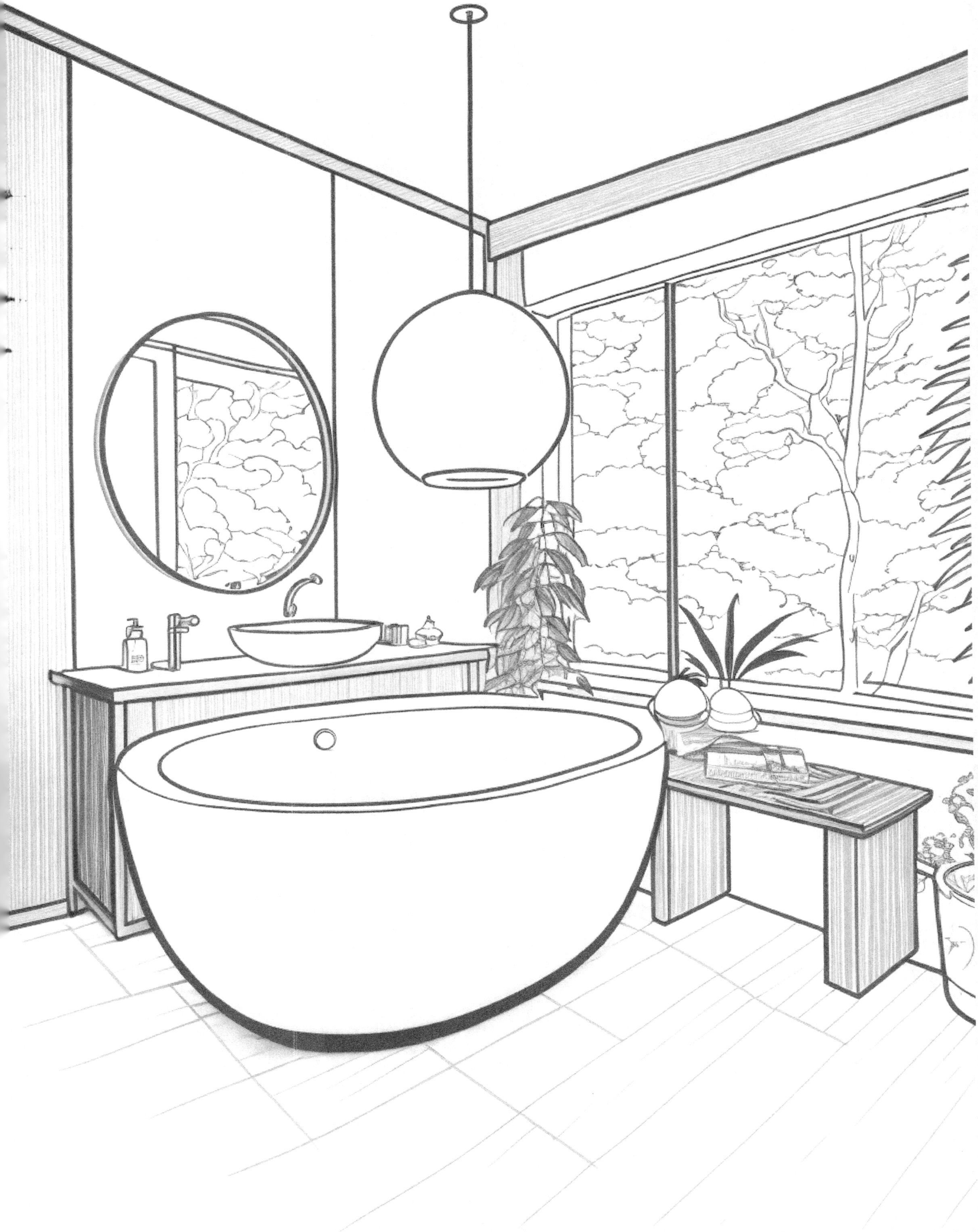

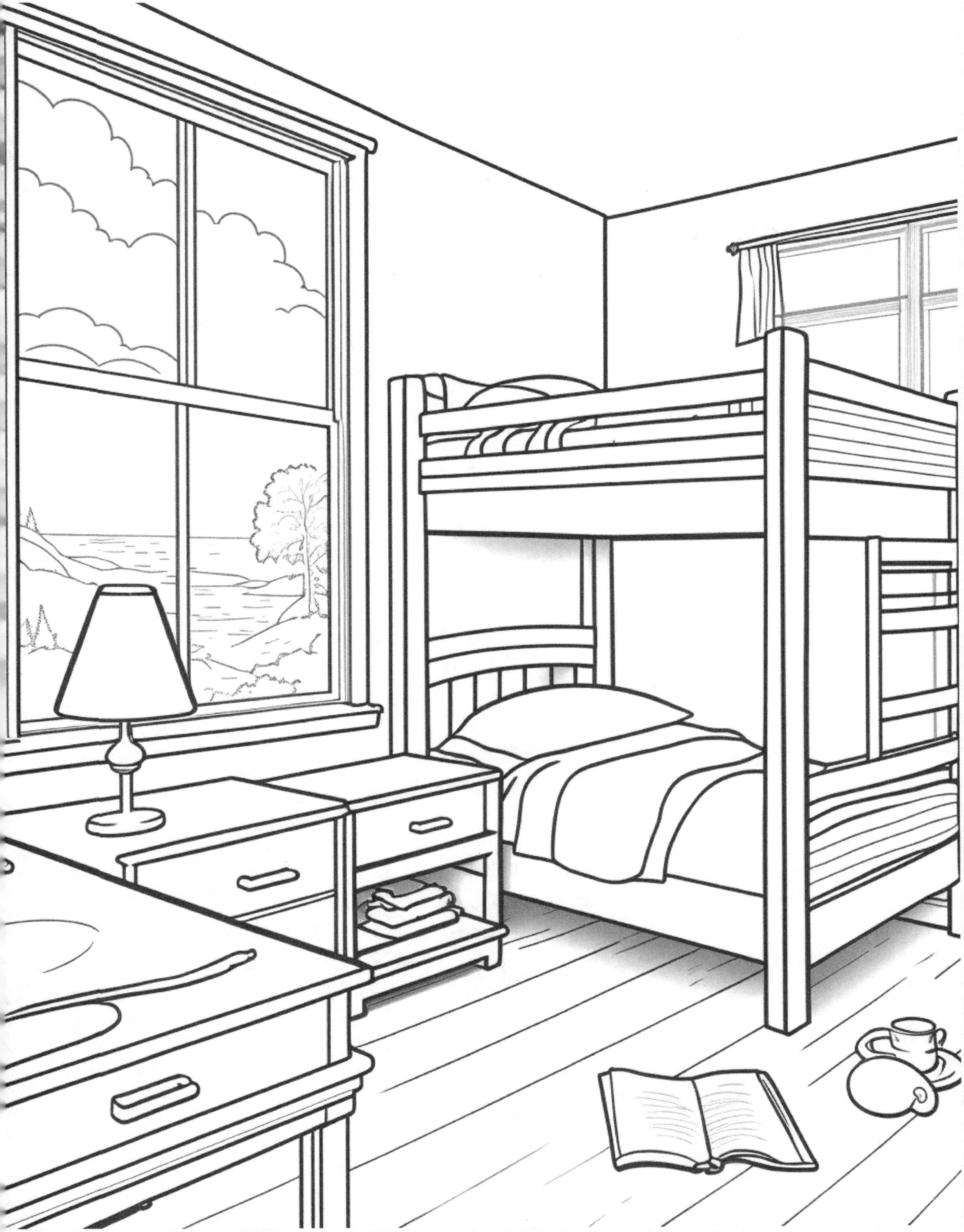

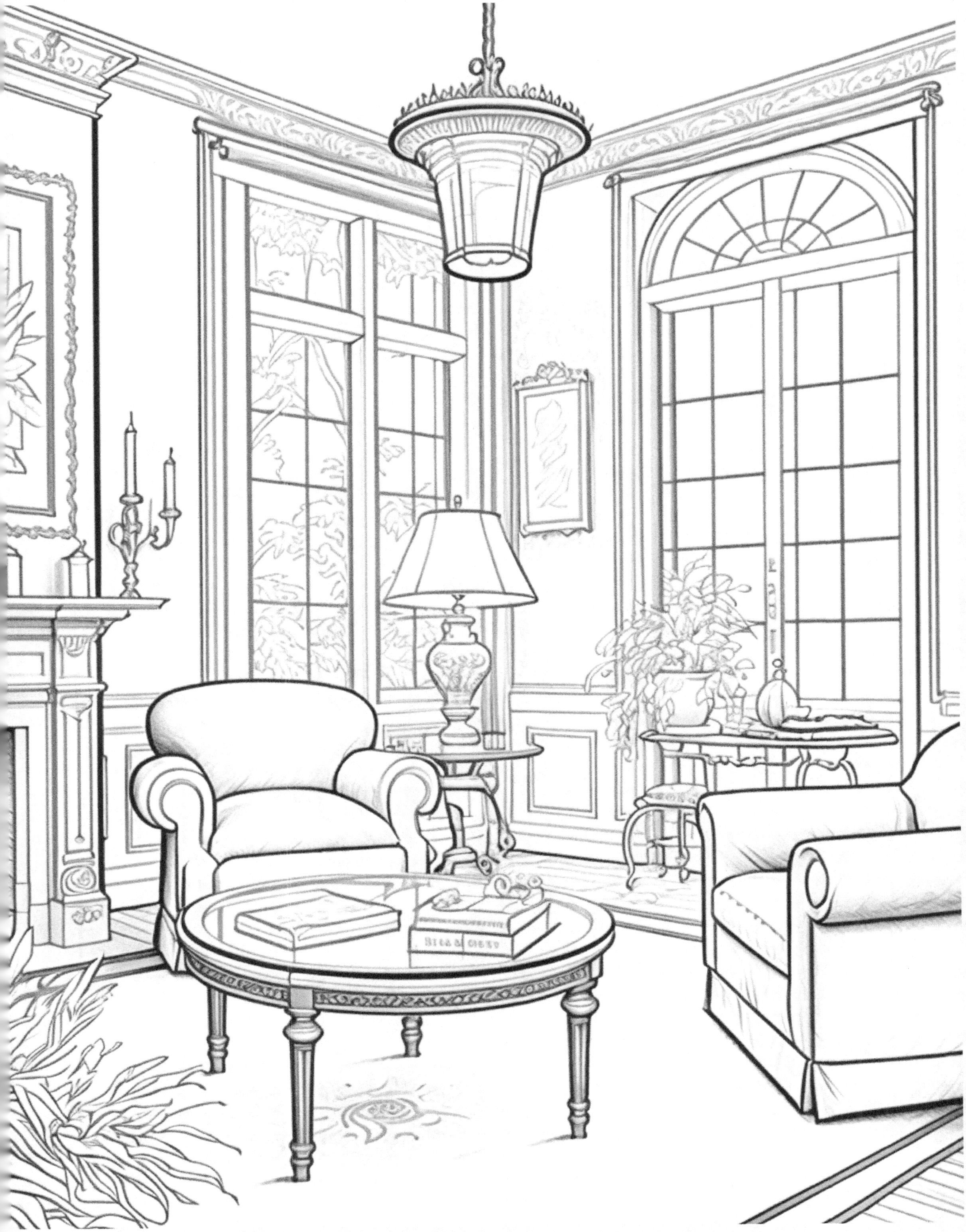

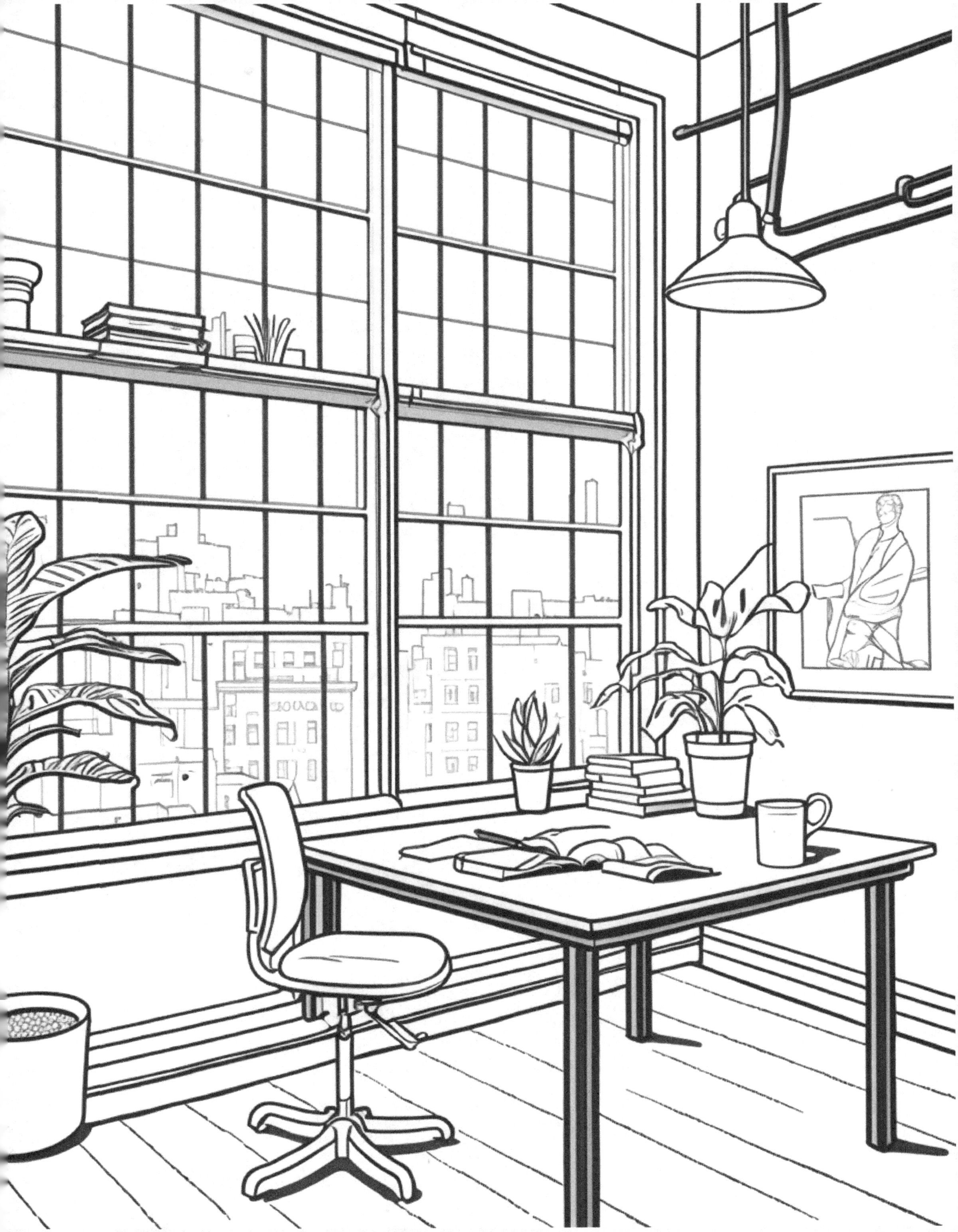

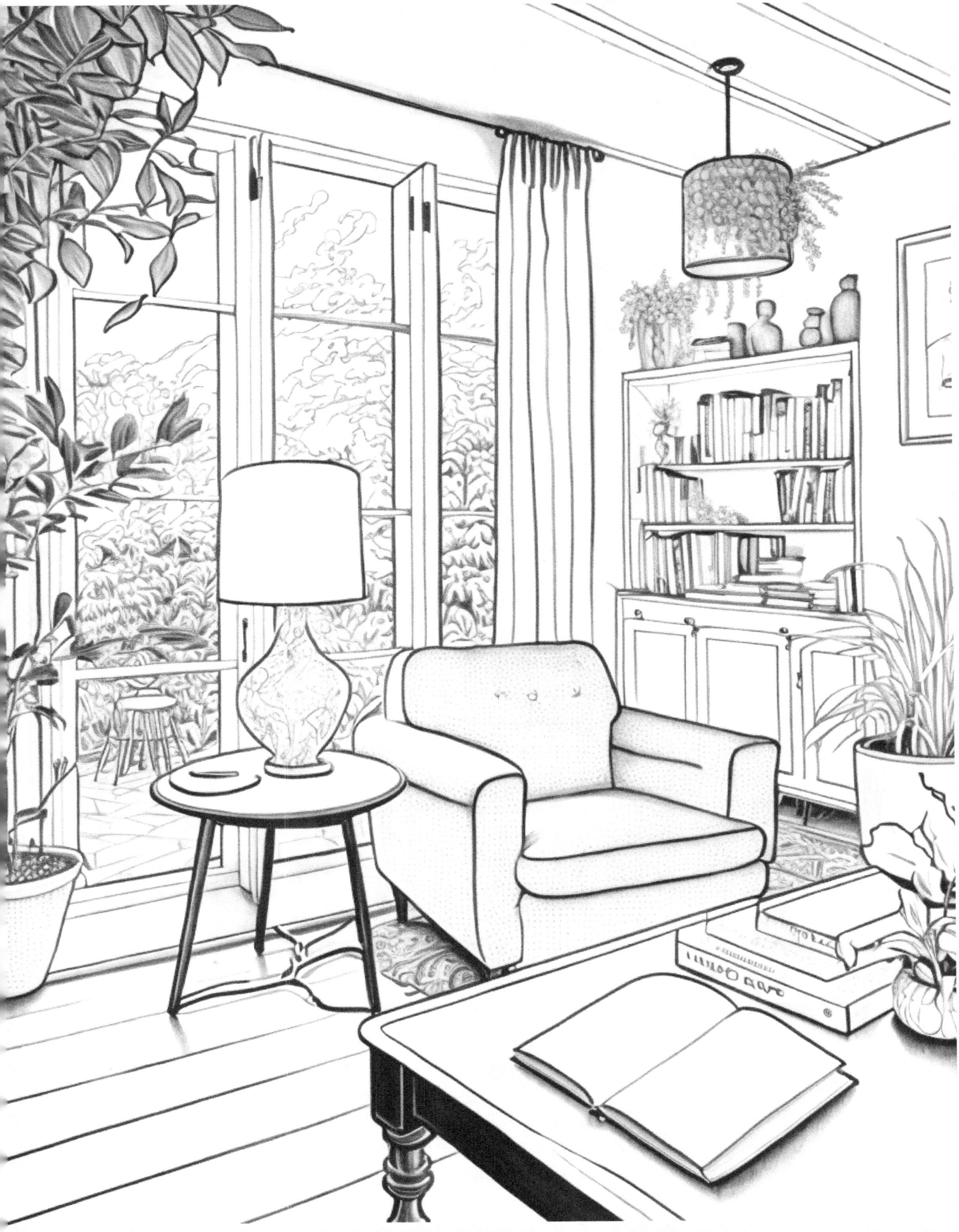

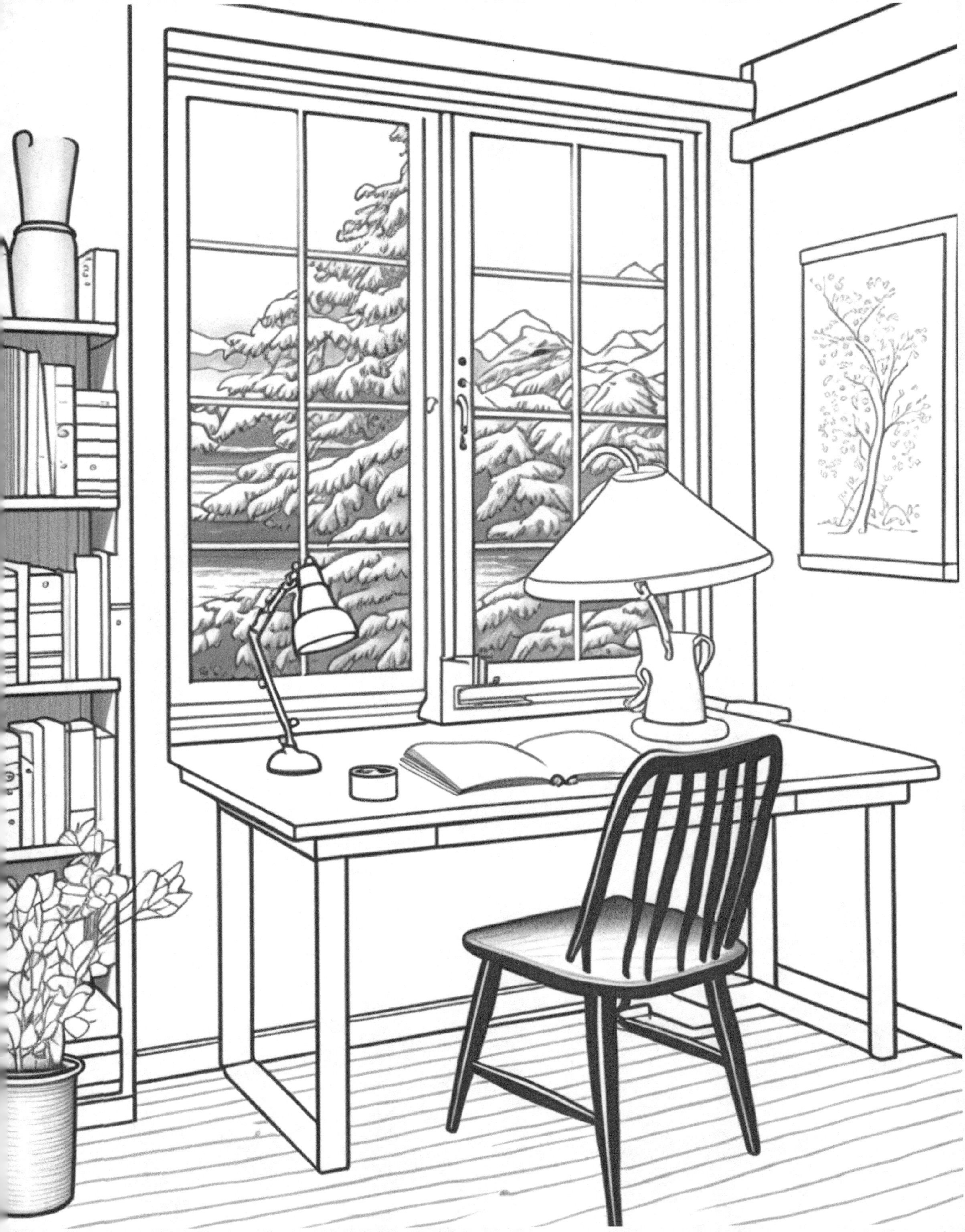

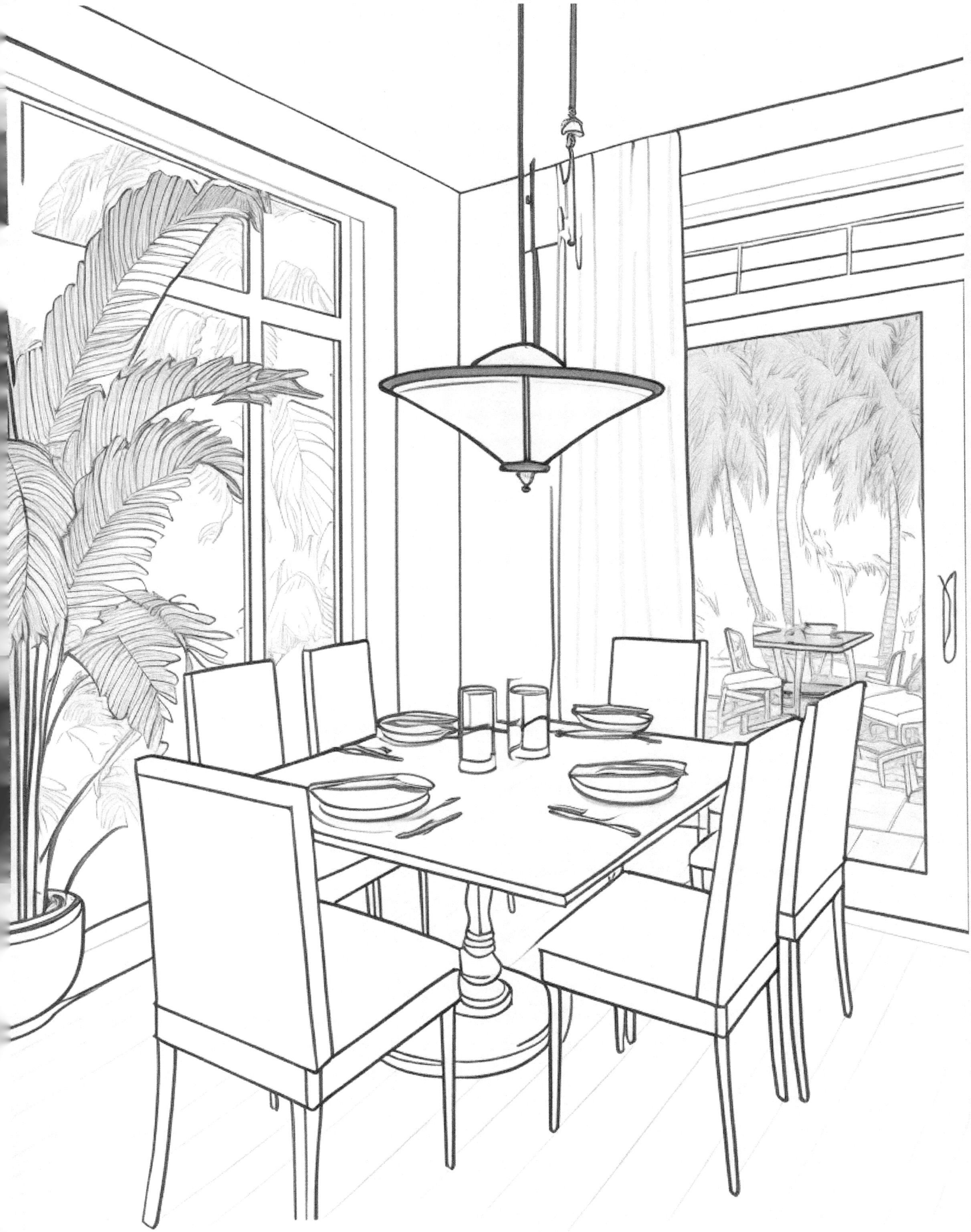

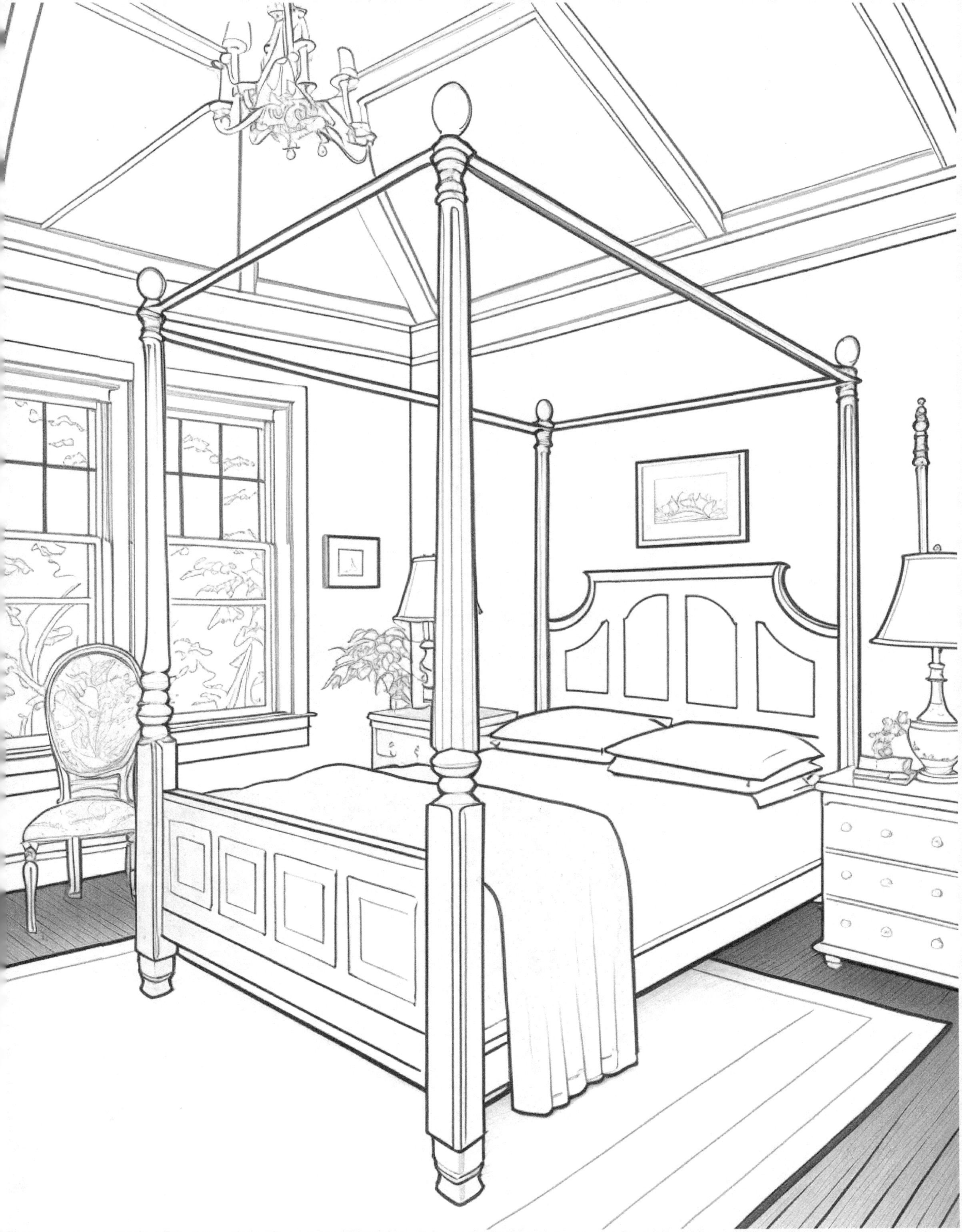

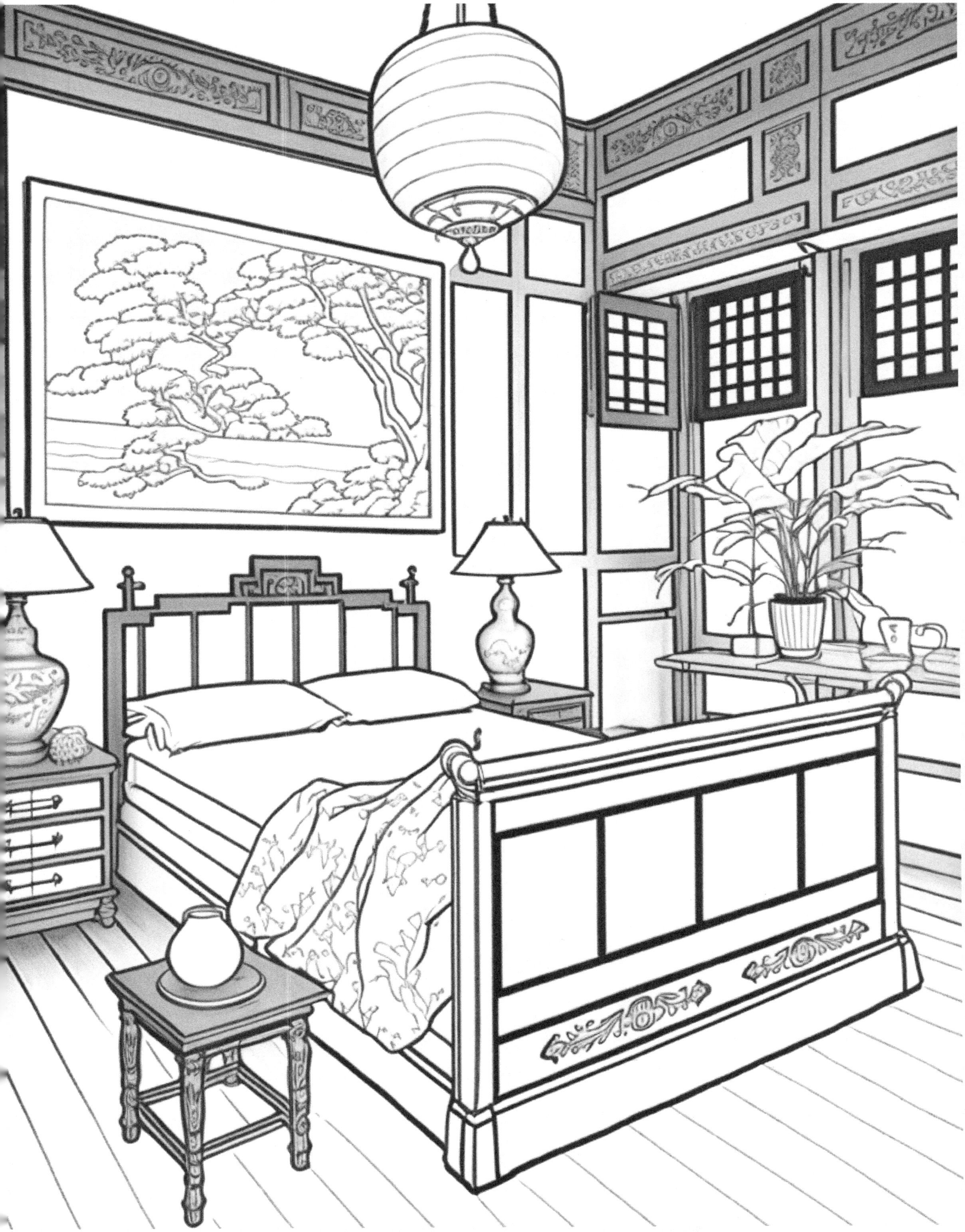

Made in the USA
Las Vegas, NV
30 November 2024

13032009R00059